MAGNIFICENT MEEKNESS

Practicing His Presence in a Secular Society

MAGNIFICENT MEEKNESS

Practicing His Presence in a Secular Society

MORTON BUSTARD

Destiny Image® Publishers, Inc.
P.O. Box 310
Shippensburg, PA 17257-0310

"Speaking to the Purposes of God for This Generation
and for the Generations to Come"

ISBN 0-7684-2072-5

For Worldwide Distribution
Printed in the U.S.A.

First Printing: 2002   Second Printing: 2002

This book and all other Destiny Image, Revival Press, MercyPlace,
Fresh Bread, Destiny Image Fiction, and Treasure House books
are available at Christian bookstores and distributors worldwide.

For a U.S. bookstore nearest you, call **1-800-722-6774**.
For more information on foreign distributors, call **717-532-3040**.
Or reach us on the Internet:
www.destinyimage.com

DEDICATION

In gratitude to my wife Marilyn,
and daughters, Datha and Kayla:
Thanks for your steadfast confidence.
I am delighted to dedicate this book to you.

CONTENTS

FOREWORD

The meek might be in line to inherit the earth, but this book is not for those without courage and strength of character. From the challenge of the Silent Lamb—questioning your submission and accountability—to the notion of Radical Restoration and its concepts of confession and confidence, Morton Bustard draws you in chapter by chapter. You will find yourself, even in the secular society in which we live, consumed by the pursuit and practice of the presence of God by the power of *Magnificent Meekness*.

Tommy Tenney
Author, GodChaser

INTRODUCTION

Magnificent Meekness pierces through dense clouds of discouragement with brilliant rays of optimism for those detained in the clutches of feeling inadequate. For anyone who has been restricted to the sidelines, this book extends an invitation to enter the arena and participate as the Church rapidly ascends to an unprecedented horizon.

Despondent souls will be exhilarated as they read of heroes with hang-ups who nonetheless were in the employment of God's Kingdom. Like medicinal ointment applied to painful lesions it will soothe those who are wounded from the virulent thorns of religion.

It not only inspires but also instructs with compassionate words of caution and counsel. After several years of ministry I find myself becoming more and more appreciative of timeless truths that have provided buoyancy amid life's unpredictable ocean. As my modest vessel has listed at times, the mast momentarily disappearing into violent breakers, these immutable principles have sustained balance.

These are not antiquated heirlooms to be exhibited in curio cabinets but rather a standard of conduct that should be practiced daily. Throughout the numerous societal changes in an ambivalent world they still remain effective. The pioneers who blazed trails that now are smooth highways understood the necessity of intimacy with God. Personally I'd like to be distinguished by the meekness of these extraordinary men and women.

When I enlisted to do the will of God, I was not motivated by grandiose dreams of fame and fortune. To me there was no ultimatum but to obey the bidding of the Holy Spirit, wherever and whatever that entailed. Those were the good ole days when starting out with one small suitcase was not uncommon.

After preaching my first sermon away from home in a small community center, God assured me He would supply every need as I endeavored to do His will. I can say without hesitation that He has been faithful.

I am a capitalist who enjoys freedom and free enterprise, but I am cognizant that prosperity must be kept in perspective. Stewardship embraces conditions that place Christ and His Church at the top of the list. As we speedily advance toward the finish line with evening shadows lengthening, emphasis must be concentrated on evangelism, not egotism.

Humility, in its truest form, is an empowering force. There is something absolutely awesome about the attitude of lowliness. Insecurities dissolve under the mantle of meekness as we seek identity in Him and not ourselves.

Chapter One

THE SILENCE
OF THE LAMB

And it came to pass, that after three days they found Him in the temple, sitting in the midst of the doctors, both hearing them, and asking them questions. And all that heard Him were astonished at His understanding and answers. And when they saw Him, they were amazed: and His mother said unto Him, Son, why hast Thou thus dealt with us? behold, Thy father and I have sought Thee sorrowing. And He said unto them, How is it that ye sought Me? wist ye not that I must be about My Father's business? And they understood not the saying which He spake unto them. And He went down with them, and came to Nazareth, and was subject unto them: but His mother kept all these sayings in her heart. And Jesus increased in wisdom and stature, and in favour with God and man (Luke 2:46-52).

What if you had some sort of foreknowledge that defined with unequivocal accuracy every aspect of your life? If all mystery had been erased and you knew everything you would do and when you would do it? If you knew precisely the range of your longevity because you were aware when you would exit this stage of life?

When Saul, the enraged, rejected king of Israel, was in hot pursuit of David, David declared to his ally Jonathan, the son of Saul, that there remained only one step between him and death (see 1 Sam. 20:3). Having access to this kind of information might cause one to reprioritize his or her life.

Things others take for granted would be cherished. Very little daylight would be burned. Everything would hold significance: from the chirping of a bird to the barking of a dog; from the artistic pigmentation of a leaf to a simple pine needle; from one's own mundane backyard to exotic regions abroad. Whether dining on a scrumptious meal in an expensive restaurant or a simple bologna sandwich in your den, you would savor every morsel. Loved ones would receive your undivided attention and you would treasure each word and every moment while in their company.

Many natural desires and yearnings would never be realized in your life. Some of the pleasures others would get to enjoy would be off-limits to you. But every emotion they experience, every element of life, and every stage of development would be painfully real to you.

You would be like a spectator who possesses all the potential to be the MVP, yet not be permitted to step onto the field. You would endure one adrenaline rush after another as you viewed the action, knowing beyond doubt that your participation would guarantee victory. It would be ridiculous to think that Tiger Woods should be confined to the gallery or Michael Jordan restricted to the bench; equally irrational would be for you to experience exemption from so many things.

I can only imagine the lures that satan, with his poisonous and insidious nature, dangled in front of Jesus. There is no way to correlate His level of temptations to ours. I take pleasure in some hobbies, but these pursuits are not likely to become a hindrance to my ministry. I enjoy pumping iron, and have been doing so for a number of years, yet I have never been tempted to take steroids. To describe what I do on the course as golfing is a misnomer. The PGA is not going to offer me a card any time soon. These activities may even perhaps humor the Lord as He watches me sweat and slice. Although others may have to keep these pastimes in perspective due to their athleticism, I feel absolutely no endangerment whatsoever.

Knowing everything about your life-to-be, you exhibit matchless honesty and integrity and would make some fortunate person a fabulous spouse, but it is not your destiny. You are without doubt the best role model a child could pattern his or her life after, but in the natural your tree bears no branches.

Foxes and fowl enjoy the security of their dwellings, but you cannot lawfully claim a place to lay your head (see Lk. 9:58), (even though you are responsible for the creation of everything from an invisible atom to the endless universe).

Some closest to you pledge their undying allegiance to you, but your foresight sees through the fragile facade of their declarations. It is disheartening to realize one day you will be forsaken and betrayed by those you cherish. What irony—having your impeccable reputation questioned by people with dubious character and depraved backgrounds.

You are incomparable but feel incomplete. You epitomize the prowess of a lion and yet the docility of a lamb. You are conscious of every chemical change, passion, and emotion in your anatomy, but some inexplicable force deep within your being merits your reverence and restraint.

The craving to please your heavenly Father preempts any desire to fulfill earthly ambitions. However, even this does not annul the part of you fashioned in the womb. Inherent appetites constantly remind you of your humanity. Every pernicious temptation contrived in hell begs for just one moment in your innocent mind.

You are the ultimate trophy that savage predators seek to capture and display in their showcase. Every move you make and every step you take is being calculated. Satan is always anxious to approach your Father with damaging accusations. Realizing you must preserve the highest level of purity, you refuse to succumb to such nefarious thoughts. Satan fails to establish even the slightest foothold in your life.

> *Hereafter I will not talk much with you: for the prince of this world cometh, and hath nothing in Me* (John 14:30).

It seems preposterous that a measly piece of lint would utterly ruin a garment; but if one speck of iniquity attaches itself to your life it will abolish the efficacy of your sacrifice.

Your purity benefits the riffraff of society, even those who will be responsible for your gory, undeserved punishment. Why does love in the first degree carry such an awful penalty?

Doesn't seem fair. One strike, you're out! Everyone loses—everyone who lived and died before you stepped foot on Earth and everyone afterward. If you drop the ball it will be as if you never existed and humanity will be left without a hope.

Contemplating the Inevitable

Due to your extraordinary fondness of the Scriptures, you constantly ingest the words of the prophets, but an eerie sensation sometimes grips you as you see a portrait of yourself in their words. The similarities are too distinct to be coincidental. The passage where an elderly man binds his teenage boy atop a heap of stones seems to arrest your attention and provoke serious thought (see Gen. 22:9).

As you peruse the pages of Moses' writings you sense this awesome feeling of a prearranged destiny. Whenever a sacrifice is referred to, you imagine the dreadful fate of the lamb, and your stomach churns with apprehension. Your thoughts become transfixed on the innocent animal being led naively to an altar. The plunging knife, trembling lamb, and crimson blood play through your mind with uncanny reality.

There is an unusual sensation that your surroundings hold some sort of symbolism that point to future events. For some reason or another, the pounding of a hammer penetrating a nail deep into wood captivates your mind. As Joseph wields the heavy mallet, the palms of your hands quiver as if they were actually feeling pain. You marvel at your fascination over such trivial things.

It is not as though you were born with a terminal illness and a prognosis denying you a full life. You are young, healthy, brilliant, and could achieve anything you set your mind to. But your days have been predetermined to total just half of those indicated in Scripture (see Ps. 90:10).

In a few years a descending dove will expose your divine identity (see Mt. 3:16-17). However, a death warrant was published long before your birth certificate was even printed. You are infinite love incarnate, but will be despised unlike any other. The inhabitants of the amoral abyss have received orders to annihilate you.

You will relinquish your life into the hideous hands of these ghastly degenerates and they will relish in your debacle. You must volunteer for this gruesome occasion because their dreadful malice is not a formidable adversary for your unfathomable compassion. It is mandatory that you enter this habitat called Hades in order to fulfill your assignment. Your safe return will be entrusted to your heavenly Father (see Ps. 16:10).

The Preteen Christ

These would be intimidating circumstances for the most stalwart man, let alone a boy not yet in his teens. However, Jesus must possess amazing resolve to be able to handle all that is on His plate. It is a juggling performance that surpasses the most ambidextrous entertainer.

Jesus must possess a growing awareness of His absolute identity. Believing that what He is presently doing is His Father's business verifies that He has discovered His place in prophecy. He is cognizant that His real Father is not the mild-mannered gentleman who instructs Him in the carpentry shop. He may address Joseph as Papa, but He knows Joseph is not His Daddy.

He harbors not a solitary rebellious intention. He is far removed from being an incorrigible brat who needs his backside tanned. He is not a juvenile delinquent who enjoys slipping out of the reach of His mother, causing her worry and panic. There is no indication of violence in His nature.

> *He is cognizant that His real Father is not the mild-mannered gentleman who instructs Him in the carpentry shop. He may address Joseph as Papa, but He knows Joseph is not His Daddy.*

A bruised reed shall He not break, and the smoking flax shall He not quench: He shall bring forth judgment unto truth (Isaiah 42:3).

Jesus has not suddenly taken a turn for the worse. He has not seized an opportunity to slip from the presence of Joseph and Mary and sow some wild oats. He is just doing what He feels He should be doing. Perhaps He can't quite put His finger on it, but this seems to be the direction that He should be taking. He is in the temple, answering and asking questions. Those in attendance, regardless of their pedigree and knowledge of Scripture, sit in awe.

This is the kind of prodigy a university would like to come in contact with. Today scholarships to the most elite institutions of higher learning would readily be made available to Him. Major corporations would be reaching out to secure Him in their circle before some other "headhunter" acquired Him.

A few of His peers admire Him, some like Him, but many despise Him due to the attention He receives. There are those who simply dismiss Him as being mysterious, kind of weird, or something. However, He refuses to reciprocate their negative opinions.

He probably feels more at home in the temple than in the workshop. This seems much more appropriate than the playground or the ballpark. He is not displaying an egotistical exhibition of His intelligence; He's just a lad trying to do what seems right.

What was so wrong with Jesus in the temple? I'm sure there were much worse places a boy His age could have frequented. I think one may have had to search diligently to find any other parents who would have been upset by having their preteen in just such an atmosphere. Citing Scriptures was certainly not a bad activity. After all, His mind easily could have been preoccupied with less wholesome interests.

I imagine that there existed ample mischief for a lad to engage in during this era. Maybe swiping a yoke of oxen, jumping into the cart, and taking a joyride through town. "Boys will be boys" and I'm certain plenty of opportunities presented themselves to Jesus as with His peers. There surely must have been a lot of yearnings that He had to suppress.

It may have been that a feeling of urgency seized Him. If for some reason His life on Earth was intended to be of short duration, mingling with this pious company would have been an ideal location to embark on the will of God.

Considering Herod's edict to assassinate infant boys at the time of Jesus' birth, His peer group was probably very limited. This, of course, would have contributed to a lonely existence. Or maybe He just grew weary of being a big brother to His younger siblings.

The Quest for Christ

When considering that Jesus had been missing from Mary and Joseph for three days, all kind of possibilities exist (see Lk. 2:46). After all, three days without parental supervision can allow for a lot of misbehavior. I'm sure a lot of questions remained to be answered when they finally located Him and the trauma ended.

I can't begin to think of my reaction in discovering that one of my daughters was unaccounted for. I would employ every means available to assist in the search. I would exhaust every avenue of possibility. If I discovered she had slipped away of her own accord, she would know the full extent of my anxiety and experience some degree of punishment.

It's a parent's most frightening nightmare—fretting over children who should be nestled under cozy blankets in bedrooms strewn with toys, instead left to the discretion of ominous nights. Mothers and fathers struggle to clench any ray of hope, at times judging themselves harshly. If only they hadn't been so stern, or if they would have given them whatever, this all would not be happening.

Here's a valid point: If Mary messes up, it's over! Now that's maternal responsibility. Where is Mary's little Lamb in this wretched world of darkness? For somewhere around 72 hours she searches for Christ.

And He said unto them, How is it that ye sought Me? wist ye not that I must be about My Father's business? (Luke 2:49)

Mary, distraught over her missing boy, enters the temple and discovers Jesus. Catching her breath, struggling to regain her composure, Mary approaches the child wonder. The Q & A session is suddenly interrupted. She demands He leave the temple immediately and accompany her and Joseph home to Nazareth. Jesus' reply: "Wist ye not that I must be about my Father's business?"

Declaring He was doing His Father's business! It is amazing how such few words can pack such a punch. It is not a case of being disrespectful. Jesus reminds Mary of the variables concerning who and what He is. He does not disavow Joseph, but simply reminds the humble guardian of His position.

Here He stands, pulled between two worlds. Deity is being disciplined. The Creator is being chastised. What do you do when you have two points of origin with each one being diametrically opposite? What is the right thing to do when you feel a tug on the right and on the left?

If anyone should have realized this boy had a heavenly mandate, Mary should have been the first. Some may have doubted His birth, but not His mother. She had no secrets to hide, no skeletons in her closet. His existence was not the result of unbridled passion producing illegitimacy. The conception of Christ was one encounter with the Holy Spirit she would never forget (see Lk. 1:35).

Maybe this was just a classic case of an overprotective mother. Was Mary out of her jurisdiction in requiring the lad to return home? Was there the possibility that this action on her part could prevent the will of God from being accomplished in Jesus' life? Would Jesus have been justified in refusing to go with Mary and Joseph? Remember, the will of God did weave its way into this scenario!

"Pack it in, you're going home, young man!" For sure He thought He was pleasing His Father, but then His mother was scolding Him. He responded with obedience, not insolence. No record of any argument, no *"But Mom!"* He simply nodded— His face may have reddened slightly in embarrassment—pivoted on His heel, and went on home. Perhaps an inner struggle began in His spirit as He wondered if He was doing the right thing in obeying Mary.

Going Back to Get Ahead

Understanding the perfect will of God is not always easy. It can be especially confusing and frustrating for someone just beginning his or her journey. What is one supposed to do when he or she senses the urgency of the hour, but yet feels a responsibility to obey what may be the voice of reason? The reality is, God places elders in our life to aid us in discerning what is right when it is too vague for us to distinguish on our own. It is up to the individual to be in submission.

> *Obey them that have the rule over you, and submit yourselves: for they watch for your souls, as they that must give account, that they may do it with joy, and not with grief: for that is unprofitable for you* (Hebrews 13:17).

To declare being the Savior of the world is an enormous assignment; considering it top priority is an understatement. How then could returning to Nazareth be the will of God? I think that one man put it perfectly in perspective: *It is not enough to be anointed, you must also be appointed.*

There are times when God sends us home and sits us down. He doesn't need us to speak up, but to hush up. It is as if we have been placed in a divine holding pattern. We implore God for answers, but Heaven's silence is deafening. This puts a strain on the moorings of our faith as we drift amid an ocean of questions.

It doesn't mean He is disappointed or upset with us. We argue and assert that the fate of lost humanity is of vital interest. This is no time to be resting when we should be reaching. There is such little time remaining, one cannot afford to squander a moment. As the world grows spiritually darker with each passing day, what benefit is there in staying home?

We loathe those one-horse, rural, and rustic Nazareths He sequesters us to. If one were going fishing, it would seem sensible to go where the fish are! When you have an anointing that can potentially shake the world, what are you doing in this rinky-dink place? After all, Christianity is colossal, not a cottage industry. If withdrawal from the main flow of society is necessary, you can think of a thousand locations more suitable, but not this armpit! It seems as though we have detoured off superhighways onto narrow roads that lead to seclusion.

Have you ever felt you were stuck in the wrong place at the wrong time? You fit in your environment about as well as a reptile in the Antarctic! You feel like an orchid that poked its head from the soil and discovered it was in a cornfield. Talk about a square peg in a round hole!

All the prayer and fasting in the world will not change the mind of God. Divine providence has arranged this hiatus in your so very important itinerary. I understand you are zealous to go forward and evangelize the world, but for now, take a few steps backward and go to school. There awaits an education in accountability that God deems necessary.

Obscure Adolescence

There have been biographies of people, written in painstaking detail, that in no way can be put on the same shelf as the pages penned about the Son of God. So as you pore over the pages, you endure the minutiae of information, from cradle to grave, but they fail to hold your interest in the least. It appears as though every event in the life of the subject has been chronicled with very few worthy of mention. Many of these tomes are never completely consumed, but end up collecting dust on a bookshelf, even though someone deemed it deserving of research and publishing.

I really don't think there exists a single moment of Jesus' life unworthy of recognition. It may be an embellishment to suggest that every millisecond should be canonized. But 18 *silent* years! Yes! For 18 years we have no record! Considering such a momentous assignment as the Redeemer of humanity, how do you account for 18 years of silence?

Evidently, accountability is that vital to God. It was absolutely *expedient* that Jesus experience humility and submit to accountability. I believe it is a facet of His humanity that should be thoroughly examined, and certainly not overlooked.

With eternity rapidly approaching, and our ransom pending, God thought it necessary for His only begotten Son to return to the tiny, unassuming hamlet called Nazareth. In the humble abode of Joseph and Mary were priceless assets meant for Jesus' acquisition.

Educating the Ingenious

And the child grew, and waxed strong in spirit, filled with wisdom (Luke 2:40a).

And Jesus increased in wisdom and stature (Luke 2:52a).

How does one attempt the task of instructing the omniscient? Can it be compared to tutoring the elderly Einstein in elementary arithmetic? Not even close! So, if something is full, how is more absorbed without causing spillage?

The word used here for *increased* comes from the Greek word *prokoptw* (prok-op'-to), to beat forward, to lengthen out by hammering as a smith forges metals. Jesus was *full of wisdom*, and yet *increased in wisdom*. Obviously He must have encountered circumstances that assisted in His personal and spiritual development.

I don't feel it violates the sacredness of the Gospels to suggest that the years, months, weeks, and days of *silence* are replete with experiences that caused Christ to *increase*. Although unwritten, His twenties must have been enlightening. Reticence does not suggest irrelevance. Each phase of life presented opportunities and opposition. He grasped the theory and incorporated the practical. He was endowed with peerless wisdom and yet saw room for further development.

His apprenticeship was not limited to an uncomplicated woodshop. His surroundings became His classroom and experiences were His teachers. Rather than swagger around with a know-it-all attitude, He listened and learned, observed and improved. He met every expectation with excellence and maximized every particle of possibility.

It is good for a man that he bear the yoke in his youth (Lamentations 3:27).

Pleasing God and Man

*And Jesus increased...in **favour** with God and man* (Luke 2:52, emphasis added).

In obeying this imposed sabbatical to Nazareth, Christ earned the favor of both God and His neighbors. He was *heavenly minded* and *earthly good*, reconciling two entirely converse spheres. He remained sanctified without becoming sanctimonious; anointed, yet not annoying.

I would speculate that Jesus was the most amiable, affectionate person who ever existed. He was Mary's pride and Joseph's partner; an outstanding resident of an unpretentious town. He was holy but not haughty, perfect but not proud.

Not a solitary unkind word slid off the tip of His tongue. His reputation was untouchable, and His honor incontestable. His demeanor conveyed compassion and His treatment of people was equal, regardless of their social ranking.

He condescended but was not condescending. He did not patronize these average people living in an inconspicuous place called Nazareth. In one part of Him, this was all He had known. Another part of Him had sat on a celestial throne and surveyed wondrous worlds in the remotest caverns of space.

He was Mary's pride and Joseph's partner; an outstanding resident of an unpretentious town. He was holy but not haughty, perfect but not proud.

Generation Xed

My personal opinion, and sincere conviction, is that if accountability is not appreciated and practiced, a young generation of ministry is traveling on a collision course. I understand that the statement, "No man is an island," is a worn-out cliché; however, as antiquated as it may be, it still carries a lot of truth.

Absalom is an excellent example of a person with great potential, the unique advantage of a regal heritage, and aspirations to an illustrious future. He had no equal when it came to good looks, and received more acclamation than any other in all of Israel (see 2 Sam. 14:25). But what a tragedy! He squandered everything, simply because he had no accountability in his life. He refused to come under the covering of his father, King David.

He erased all the wonderful things that could have been written of him as well as obliterated any future for his offspring. There is little doubt that the final chapter of his life would have read much differently if he would have been in subjection to his father. His defining characteristic is insubordination. Although rebellion took him to the gate of the city (see 2 Sam. 15:2), accountability would have afforded him the throne over Israel.

Instead of raising up a son, he is accredited with a stone. A sad commentary on a would-be-king turned loser: no prospective princes, just a pillar of stone, authenticating his existence. Mere speculation exists over the fate of his three sons. Somewhere they dissipated into the vague shadows of obscurity, never again to be mentioned. He abdicated the monarchy over insurgence, not for a seductive siren.

> *Now Absalom in his lifetime had taken and reared up for himself a pillar, which is in the king's dale: for he said, I have no son to keep my name in remembrance: and he called the pillar after his own name: and it is called unto this day, Absalom's place* (2 Samuel 18:18).

One of the primary reasons gangs control many of our schoolyards and streets in America is the lack of fathers in homes. Some careless man proved his manhood by impregnating a woman, but wasn't man enough to stick around. The reality of a child's growing up with a single parent—maybe no parent—didn't seem significant to him. Our blessed country promoted unrestrained sex and now we are paying a premium price.

"My concern is that we are now embarked upon an experiment that violates a universal social law: In attempting to raise children without two parents, we are seeing on a massive scale, the voluntary breakup of the minimal family unit. This is historically unprecedented, an authentic cultural revolution—and, I believe, socially calamitous."[1] William Bennett went on further to say, "As the long record of human experimentation attests, civilizations, even great civilizations, are more fragile and perishable than we think."[2]

God doesn't need gang-bangers in His Kingdom—people equipped with supernatural gifts, tapping into bottomless financial reservoirs, but having not a single, solitary elder to answer to—a perfect example of digging one's own grave. Mark it down, there will be confusion and casualties. Before the ink dries on the freshly printed news page, the presses will start up again, reporting stories that bring reproach on the Church. But what the comely Bride of Christ, the glorious Church, doesn't need is another scandal, bringing distress and disgrace.

The words of a dear friend reverberate through the corridors of my mind: "The final chapter on any of our lives has not yet been written." The Scripture affords no ambiguity when it states: "Better is the end of a thing than the beginning thereof: and the patient in spirit is better than the proud in spirit" (Eccles. 7:8).

Building River Banks and Mending Fences

A river without banks is a swamp, the characteristics of which do not impress me. It is a breeding ground for fatal disease such as malaria. A swamp has very little depth, and because it doesn't flow, has absolutely no force. It is just a pool of motionless, stagnated, contaminated water, swarming with mosquitoes.

If a river has banks that undergo erosion, then not only will the levees deteriorate, but the river will be reduced to a rill. Currents that at one time rotated the enormous turbines of a hydroelectric dam, generating vast quantities of electricity, become stationary, and thus unproductive.

One summer I witnessed a magnificent river brought to a standstill. While ministering in eastern Arkansas I beheld the mighty Mississippi as dry as a bone. Barges laden with tons of freight, and propelled by powerful tugs, were brought to an abrupt halt atop sandbars. Alternate means of exportation had to be employed since no natural means existed to empower the river.

We can apply the characteristics of a stagnant, stale body of water to our own lives. For people to possess depth and power in the Kingdom they need disciplines, such as guardrails that run parallel to life's highway. Embankments on both sides are necessary to direct the rushing current all the way to the sea, as the river continuously empties into something much larger than itself.

Pouring back into oneself is entirely self-absorbent, and will negate a future of any substantial length. Whether the collar is white, blue, or clergy, it is imperative for everyone to be connected to something larger than him or herself.

No member of the Body of Christ is autonomous from the rest of the various multitudes that comprise the Kingdom of God. No ministry, regardless of enormity and effectiveness, is separate from its workers, who labor for the eternal cause.

Mainstream charismatic circles need to reestablish a conservation program. It is time to deal with issues that have been neglected. There is a mentality that contends that disciplines are no longer applicable for today. Attention had better be placed on eroding shorelines before an unprecedented drought of spirituality occurs. The current may not appear to be slowing, nor the depth decreasing. However, in due time the ebb and flow will cease to turn the immense wheel of the gristmill.

On the other end of the spectrum, when banks contract too close, another problem is created: overflow. We do not need totalitarianism. I have known young men and women who were victims of such oppressive leadership: collateral damage from political rancor.

Denominations that attempt to sustain their religious citadels by corralling constituents are instead squeezing them out. It is obvious the world is rejecting centralized government; the Church should sit up and take notice.

Because we are human, we need perimeters. Our neighbors may be benevolent and upstanding citizens, but we still must have boundaries. Barriers are not always negative blockades. They can serve both the neighbor's and the landowner's best interest by keeping both parties in check. We may not go to the extent of fencing off our acreage, but we are aware of a plat registered in the county courthouse that verifies ownership.

Take caution when you dismantle all the fence rails and fence posts along the margins of your life. You may receive the rude awakening that the greener grass on the other side is actually

Astroturf! The aesthetics may suggest authenticity but eventually will prove to be simply a substitute for the genuine. This may be practicable for a ballgame, but remember, this isn't a game!

Good Leaders Follow

For more than 20 years I have been in a leadership position. Any success I have experienced can be attributed to the fact that I have always placed my ministry under a ministry. Good leaders have mentors. They are continually improving their skills by surrounding themselves with people who have surpassed them. Don't take yourself so seriously. The people you lead can only go as far as you take them. If you don't continue to guide and direct, it won't be long until you will be out of a job. Your students will eventually catch up to you, probably sooner than later.

I constantly stay in touch with elders who are in covenant with me. I have afforded them the liberty of having access into every part of my ministry, including financial aspects. These checks and balances assist in keeping me in proper alignment.

Recently I sought council from an elder concerning an opportunity that had presented itself. An invitation had inadvertently been extended to me to minister at a prestigious assembly. The church had merited worldwide acclaim and would have granted my ministry vast exposure. However, the elder admonished me that the timing was not correct.

The subject became moot. I cannot preach and write on accountability and not be in submission to wise council myself. My nature is not always such for me to acquiesce so quickly. On several occasions I have not agreed with the advice offered, but after much thought and prayer I've conceded.

I preach that the blessings of the Lord make rich, but prosperity must be kept in perspective. I am an advocate of spiritual ministry and concur with Moses who said, "Would God that all the Lord's people were prophets, and that the Lord would put His spirit upon them" (Num. 11:29b). But perish the thought we have ministers with no mentors.

There is a surplus of material available on wealth, health, and becoming a mega-church. There are competent instructors who conduct workshops that enhance marriage, ministry, and music. I am not in the least suggesting these are trivial subject matters, but I do weep over the deficit of data available on prophetic covering, accountability, and submission.

> *For though ye have ten thousand instructors in Christ, yet have ye not many fathers: for in Christ Jesus I have begotten you through the gospel* (1 Corinthians 4:15).

The apostle who educated us on spiritual gifts and their proper operation, took spiritual fatherhood upon himself and made it a strategic part of his ministry. Timothy, Onesimus, Marcus, John Mark, and Demas were all tutored by Paul.

The God-Man

My meager attempt to depict the mystery of godliness through the medium of vocabulary lacks sufficiency. The most astute doctors of divinity with their theological terminology fall so terribly short of encompassing the Christ. He is the Lamb and the Lion, the Lily and the Rose, the Bread and the Water, the Branch and the Tree, the Sacrifice and the High

Priest, the Mediator and the Judge, the First and the Last. All of this phraseology captures a facet of the Great Eternal Wonder. However, the full revelation will not emerge in a synagogue, sanctuary, or seminary, but when we behold Him face to face.

Before Socrates, Plato, Galileo, or Guttenburg, there was God. Before the Wright brothers, jet propulsion, and space shuttles, there was God. Long before Columbus exited the court of Isabella in 1492; set sail with the Niña, Pinta, and the Santa Maria, bound for the Lesser Antilles; and ultimately set foot on the shores of the New World, there was God. And that God was very much a part of Jesus.

He was sinless, *yet was baptized*; perfect yet praying; omnipotent and yet obedient. If there was the slightest indication of reluctance on the part of Jesus in returning to Nazareth, it was for a noble cause. It was certainly not because He considered Himself too sophisticated for this tiny town.

Saving Jesus

There is no insinuation in the Scriptures that Jesus as much as whispered a white lie and required redemption. He didn't necessitate a pardon but He definitely needed protection. Vanishing for three days was totally irresponsible. The boy was "Hell's Most Wanted."

Jesus thought He was pleasing His Father; instead He was distressing His momma. He thought He was doing a *God thing*. Mary actually did the *God thing*. Jesus was wise but wrong. He didn't step into sin; He walked away from safety. Mary did more than reprove Him that day in the temple. Not only did she retrieve Him, she rescued Him.

This provokes a question: How many potential power-houses could have been salvaged if they would have heeded the Marys in their lives? There are numerous examples of men and women who were selected but not elected. When they were told to wait, they went. The wisest council in the world failed to convince them the timing was not right.

A pattern of Jesus' submission begins with His obedience to Mary, which stayed with Him throughout His earthly existence. Somewhere amid those silent years Jesus learned the value of accountability.

Then answered Jesus and said unto them, Verily, verily, I say unto you, The Son can do nothing of Himself, but what He seeth the Father do: for what things soever He doeth, these also doeth the Son likewise (John 5:19).

Although He was God manifest in flesh, there was a part of Him that necessitated growth. God intends that all His children be involved in the maturation process. He doesn't want His sons and daughters to become spiritual pigmies; rather He wants them to attain stature and depth.

Grow for It

Now I say, That the heir, as long as he is a child, dif-fereth nothing from a servant, though he be lord of all; but is under tutors and governors until the time appointed of the father (Galatians 4:1-2).

Imagine the absurdity of someone submitting an application for a position requiring a degree of expertise to a Fortune 500 company, and when asked for credentials, sliding a birth certificate across the personnel officer's desk. It happens repeatedly in the Kingdom. There is a high percentage of people who have failed to make it beyond the nursery.

Maturity is achieved through discipline. Those who reject instruction rob themselves of experiencing the various stages of development. In many cases churches are not healthy organisms—ministering to their community, but amusement parks—catering to the immature. The introverted focus of these recreation centers prevents revival and expansion of God's Kingdom.

> *For when for the time ye ought to be teachers, ye have need that one teach you again which be the first principles of the oracles of God; and are become such as have need of milk, and not of strong meat* (Hebrews 5:12).

Sometimes the only way I know I am growing is due to the cool evenings. It is not because of an atmospheric or seasonal change, but rather because my coat no longer fits me properly. So, for a few months out of the year I will experience discomfort, but I'll receive a new one at the beginning of the next, just as Samuel did (see 1 Sam. 2:19).

The Monotony of Discipline

It must have been monotonous beyond definition for Jesus to have to adhere to the school system of His day. One part of Him was learning phonics, verb conjugation, and sentence structure, while another part of Him could speak words that would create worlds and author the best-seller of all time.

Can you imagine Jesus' learning simple arithmetic, addition, subtraction, and division, while another facet of His being completely comprehended quantum physics, advanced algebra, trigonometry, and calculus? He could cite precisely the distance between any two objects in outer space and their respective distances from earth.

Biology must have been a particular bore. As He grew He learned proper hygiene, basic human anatomy, and general health; yet He understood microbiology—every convoluted physical, physiological, and psychological detail.

One cannot imagine what it must have been like doing the 9 to 5 routine in an uncomplicated carpentry shop, working with the material that would one day suspend His bludgeoned body between Heaven and earth.

He integrated Himself into the very fiber of the world He came to redeem. He had hopes, dreams, and great aspirations. On a few occasions He most likely struggled with these, but for 18 years He increased. More than half of His earthly life was lived in that little Middle Eastern village. The Ancient of Days subjected Himself to a primitive civilization and was adherent to its customs and culture.

He left the temple with Mary and Joseph and made no appearance—not so much as a syllable from His mouth is recorded—until He appeared on the banks of Jordan (see Mt. 3:13). During this time of silence His cousin John the Baptist was visible. As Jesus remained anonymous, John's thundering voice echoed through the wilderness.

Throughout the span of Christ's life we find Him accountable and submissive. He would not be intimidated to perform a miracle on behalf of the Pharisees, or satan himself. A need in itself did not initiate His divine virtue; but in perceiving the presence of faith and with the permission of His Father, He then proceeded to heal.

He even submitted Himself to humanity's greatest adversary: death. If He could not sin, how could He be tempted? If He could not refuse His predestined fate, how could Calvary be a sacrifice? To suggest He lost his life denies His *laying it down* (see Jn. 10:18); to suggest He spilled His blood implies an accident.

And being found in fashion as a man, He humbled Himself, and became obedient unto death, even the death of the cross (Philippians 2:8).

Greater than any general who ever commanded an army and entrusted with more authority than the most threatening tyrant, the Invincible made Himself vulnerable. He disappeared once again for three days. Only this time He defeated satan rather than debated Scripture. Just like before, He went on home—not to a rural community, but to a royal celebration.

Though He were a Son, yet learned He obedience by the things which He suffered (Hebrews 5:8).

Chapter Two

THE AWESOME POWER
OF WEAKNESS

Then Abraham fell upon his face, and laughed, and said in his heart, Shall a child be born unto him that is an hundred years old? and shall Sarah, that is ninety years old, bear? (Genesis 17:17)

Former heavyweight boxing champion George Foreman became the purveyor of hope to all middle-aged men when he decided to reenter the ring at age 40. Senator John Glenn raised more than a few eyebrows when it was announced he would board the shuttle Discovery and return to space at age 77. Of course his colleague on the other side of the aisle, Strom Thurmond, probably wasn't all that impressed. I hear the Smithsonian of American History is giving up on procuring the venerable politician. And then there was Hulda Crooks who climbed Mount Fuji at age 91. She knew nothing about this arduous form of recreation until late in life.

Some people have the ability to disregard the date on their birth certificate. Take Nick for example. He's 62 years old and for a senior is in great shape. I have worked out with Nick for eight years. He tells me one of his secrets is his breakfast—oatmeal. Perhaps I should inquire as to which brand he buys. Allow me an attempt at satire: Maybe ole Nick is *juicin'* (a little lingo from the gym meaning "using steroids")! Or maybe I have stumbled onto the identity of the *Energizer Bunny.*

Most days I have to talk myself into finishing my exercise program. Somewhere around the halfway mark I get this overwhelming urge to bail. I guess it's called hitting the wall. I'm wondering if my endorphins have taken a permanent leave of absence. Then I see Nick aggressively pursuing his physical fitness goals. He won't be substituting for Arnold Schwarzenegger any time soon, but he still completes his rigorous two-hour routine at least three times a week.

After spotting Nick there is no way I can quit. I can't let this dinosaur outdo me. So I swipe off sweat and grudgingly get after it, doing extra repetitions so he won't make me look quite so bad. Pound for pound, considering his age, Nick is probably the strongest man in our gym. He's been a great incentive in my pursuit of physical fitness. Observing Nick makes aging at least tolerable.

Now let's consider Abraham. He had been walking around for almost a century when God reminded him that His covenant had no expiration date. Just when Abraham thought he would go to the grave carrying unfulfilled promises with him, God stepped in.

Can you imagine how the front page would have read if the *Enquirer* magazine had been in circulation in Abraham's day? I have read some headlines that were hilarious and others that were positively ridiculous. This story would have undoubtedly come under both categories.

SENIOR CITIZEN COUPLE GIVES BIRTH TO BOUNCING BABY BOY, DAD IS 100, MOM IS 90

Quite a commotion had been created as a result of the new toddler. All the old men in town were strutting like stallions. Their wives retorted, "Don't even think about it." Isn't there an old saying, "Just because there is snow on the chimney..."? Talk about discovering the *fountain of youth*.

Running the risk of being crude let me interject that this happened thousands of years before the medical breakthroughs that produced fertility pills. An interesting case study for obstetricians; even Robert Ripley, had he been around, wouldn't have believed it.

Seeing Sarah in her third trimester would have been extremely amusing. Frail legs, knobby knees, shriveled skin, and appearing to have engorged a melon. And soon after, she sat nursing Isaac. You decide whether or not God has a sense of humor.

This was an enormous interruption for a husband and wife who could have been living on social security for 30 years had it been available; no lounging around in some exotic Middle Eastern retirement community for Abraham and Sarah. Leisurely days of golfing with geezers and quilting bees were postponed; it was time to get back to work.

I have yet to encounter anyone today who can thoroughly understand the magnitude of this miracle. Several ecstatic moms and dads have testified to me of how God blessed the fruit of their womb even though it was medically impossible to conceive. However, the particulars surrounding the birth of Isaac put it in a league of its own.

I enjoy engaging my imagination over this unique trio. There's mom and dad lying on the angora rug, romping with Isaac, and then it becomes an aerobic workout to get back on their feet. I wonder who drifted off to sleep in the rocking chair first. My money is on the parents. *Rock-a-bye baby in the treezzzzzzzz.*

Changing diapers must have been interesting. Poor little Isaac probably looked like a pincushion with tiny scabs scattered on his bottom. *Hold shtill shonny, ouch, I've got it, ouch, I'm shorry, ouch, I know that hurt but momma's almosht done.*

It's a good thing Abraham had servants; I can't picture him running to catch a ball. Were there birds and bees in existence when Abraham was a boy? I mean, we're talking a while back and I'm not sure which came first.

The euphoria that emerged in that modest tent at the fulfillment of the promise must have been remarkable. To know your name will conclude with your passing and then to have an heir step into your vanishing life is almost too good to be true. Time is no longer spent reflecting on the past but instead by squeezing every drop of goodness from the present. I'm sure, due to the circumstances, they delicately held each moment as if it were a costly and fragile jewel.

A son asked his elderly dad why he awoke so early each morning. The seasoned gentleman replied, "I don't know just how many more sunrises I'll get to see. I don't want to miss a one." I'm sure this is the attitude Abraham and Sarah exhibited each day with Isaac. Living in their twilight years, and having had taken so long to get him, they didn't want to squander a moment.

Each evening they must have stood in the doorway of Isaac's room to catch a final glimpse of their son before they retired for the night. Unspeakable gratitude filled their hearts as they beheld the sleeping child. A heartwarming scene unfolds in my mind.

As Abraham lays his arm gently across Sarah's shoulders and draws her close, their eyes turn from the lad to each other. He utters a newly-wed "I love you"; she smiles, they back away and off to bed. At this stage of life, mornings are not guaranteed, and each day is considered borrowed time. He's the first thing on their minds in the morning. Every sunrise is another glorious occasion to spend time with Isaac.

Any question of God's faithfulness has been erased. The arduous trek to get here has been forgotten. The joy is indescribable, the promise undeniable. The old man's faith has been solidified and there remains nothing for which he can't believe.

Why would God choose such an elderly pair for the inception of the Jewish people? Surely other possibilities existed. My preference would have been a 30-year-old man with his beautiful olive-skinned bride aspiring to have children. Their lives are ahead of them, they can provide financial security for the lad and be present for most of his life.

This seems much more reasonable to me. However, God doesn't work in the area of what's reasonable. He does not calculate the numbers, consider the dimensions, or contemplate the dynamics and logistics to see if something is possible. *Possibility* is far below rudimentary and is totally inconsequential to Jehovah.

Panicking Over Promises

The science of the supernatural is simple but inexplicable. Sounds contradictory, but let me clarify; I can't explain how a miracle happens but I know why it happens. If I believe in God, all things are possible. That is the extent to which I can expound on the subject. Understanding the governing factors doesn't hinder or help being the recipient of a miracle. The summation is: "Have faith in God" (Mk. 11:22b).

Divine intervention would have been required had it been intended for Abraham and Sarah to conceive at ages 75 and 65, when they received the promise of an heir. But for 25 years their faith was put to the test and Abraham "staggered not at the promises of God" (Rom. 4:20a).

In the process of waiting for the fulfillment, Sarah became anxious because she feared time was running out. Once again, when we think with the carnal mind, we produce carnal remedies. She panicked over the promise and prompted Abraham to conceive with Hagar, her Egyptian handmaid, and Ishmael was born (see Gen. 16:1-4). This boy would eventually be blessed but not selected as the heir to the promise.

In Genesis chapter 16, Ishmael is born. In the next chapter Ishmael is 13 years old. In this span of time there exists no record of God talking with Abraham. Earthly solutions produce heavenly silence. God leaves us to contend with the works of our hands.

God wasn't waiting on Himself; He was waiting on Abraham. Finally, when Abraham reached 99 years of age God reintroduced Himself to Abraham as El-Shaddai, which means the *Almighty God*. It seems that God was saying to Abraham, "You've seen Me as a mighty God but now you're going to know Me as the Almighty. Now that your seed has died in your loins and you can't produce another Ishmael, no matter who the lady is, I am coming on the scene to do what you don't have the power to do.

Fertility without virility equals nothing. Sometimes it takes us a while to arrive at the place called *nothing*. This is where we have depleted all of our resources and yet remain unproductive. When we have eliminated every option and labor in vain, we have reached that desolate location called *nothing*. *So what's the point?* you ask. *Nothing* is the only matter God needs to do *something*. Since *nothing* is impossible with God there will always be *something*.

> *For with God nothing shall be impossible* (Luke 1:37).

Acknowledging the Almighty

El-Shaddai is waiting to be invited to church. I am not proposing a new theological slant. He is the same God we worship but in a greater manifestation. God has the incredible ability to transpose Himself for every situation, and to accommodate the hardiest spiritual appetite. Paul explained that it is the same Spirit who operates all the gifts in diversities of manifestations (see 1 Cor. 12:4).

I believe it is entirely possible for some to know God in a lesser or greater dimension than others know Him. There are those who are not open to revelation; they are satisfied with a traditional impression of God, an enigmatic supreme Being, but do not know Him personally. Others venture further and have an experience, but soon plateau. The fact remains, in this life we mortals will never witness God at His zenith (see Eph. 3:20).

We may have seen a measure of the manifest presence of God, but I am not aware of a church in North America that is having a divine encounter with El-Shaddai. Within the past ten years there have been phenomenal occurrences in some churches. A word of caution: Let's be careful what we designate as holy ground lest our shrines become our sepulchres. There is a move of God that will cause everything up to the present to look like a splash beside a tsunami. There comes a time when we must don our shoes and hit the trail; the fire that once illuminated the bush has vanished. It was a landmark in our journey, but not our destiny.

We erect mega-sanctuaries with congregations in the multiplied thousands. But if Almighty God shows up, instead of hiring an architectural firm to design a new complex, we will be going to the industrial parks of our cities and leasing commercial warehouses. When the Lord of the harvest partners with us in our cultivation endeavors, bumper crops will create a collision in the field (see Amos 9:13). Talk about *Miracle Grow*! The day you plant the seed the combines will come through, gleaning the crops.

We will witness the time, right here in America, when churches will be established in one day. Even now if Solomon the sage could step into this side of Calvary and stroll into one of our red-hot Holy Ghost meetings, he would undoubtedly stroke his beard and say, "Astounding! I thought it was extraordinary in my day" (see 2 Chron. 7:1-2; Hag. 2:9).

Standard Equipment

When we understand that the gifts of the Spirit are no longer an option to having revival, but standard equipment, we will experience unprecedented increase. A good illustration is when Jesus ministered to the woman at Jacob's well.

The disciples had gone to town to purchase meat. (Twelve men going shopping! Wow! That's a lot of meat!) The first thing we must do is dismiss our judgmental attitudes. Jesus peered into the woman's soul as if He was reading from a book. She was so amazed, she dropped her pitcher and headed back home.

The disciples returned and so did the woman, along with her friends. Jesus assured them that nature inhibited Him not in the least; within a brief moment of time Jesus sowed a seed and then came the harvest. The woman found a new source of water; the disciples learned of a different kind of meat.

Say not ye, There are yet four months, and then cometh harvest? behold, I say unto you, Lift up your eyes, and look on the fields; for they are white already to harvest (John 4:35).

The Battleground of the Mind

Secular humanistic reasoning has gained access into our committee meetings espousing intellectualism, prescribing natural solutions to solve spiritual matters. We've contrived multistep programs that affect everything from problems to prosperity. I am going to take the plunge and sound radical; there is nothing insoluble to the Holy Spirit. The Holy Spirit is not limited to verbal expression in a celestial dialect. It is the overcoming, triumphant, life-giving power of God. The properties of the Kingdom are righteousness, peace, and joy in the Holy Ghost (see Rom. 14:17).

Our excuses become crutches used to bolster our justification for a shortage of the miraculous. If we don't share the convictions of cessationists, where is the glory? Our illegitimate descendants bear striking resemblance to the genuine article and exhibit many of the right characteristics. However, the world is growing increasingly weary of counterfeit Christianity. Satan relentlessly endeavors to get us to accept a facsimile, something just short of authentic. He does an outstanding task of replicating the original.

Look at the parallel: Isaac and Ishmael, Esau and Jacob—flesh and spirit at variance with each other. My carnality is my worst enemy. It constantly screams for recognition and is in opposition to my spirit. Historically, it has been my experience, that just as I am about to receive the blessing, I am confronted with something bogus.

> *But as then he that was born after the flesh persecuted him that was born after the Spirit, even so it is now* (Galatians 4:29).

> *There is a way which seemeth right unto a man; but the end thereof are the ways of death* (Proverbs 14:12).

Is This That?

But this is that which was spoken by the prophet Joel (Acts 2:16).

Perhaps a limited quantity of cynicism could prove healthy. We need a visitation of the Holy Spirit, not hysteria and hypnosis. If something is learned through observation, don't feign it to be revelation. There is a difference between deduction and discernment, manipulation and manifestation. It is imperative we have spirituality and not spiritualism.

Scripture must be the measure by which we judge manifestations. I fear that much approval has been rendered just because something felt good. If feelings become our prerequisite then we are indeed extremely vulnerable. Jumping ahead in our story, Isaac was sure he was caressing the brawny, hairy hands of Esau. *Yes sir, that's him all right*. Wrong! (see Gen. 27:15-25)

Sorry to be the party-pooper, but I'd like to make a query: If the gifts of the Spirit are a sovereign demonstration of God, how can one promise prophecy upon payment? For example, if I sow a thousand-dollar seed I will receive a personal *word*! Caution: This ice is hairline thin, with hypothermic waters of deception beneath; few who take the plunge ever resurface.

If we're not careful we will become so desperate and hungry that we will swallow anything, regardless if it is fit for spiritual consumption. The Church should not resemble an MLM (multilevel market). When we start charging fees for our gifting we are flirting with the spirit of Simon the sorcerer (see

Acts 8:9-23). We are as guilty as the crooks in the temple, selling doves for penitence (see Mt. 21:12-13).

True prophets are not pre-occupied with possessions. It's no wonder they seem a little mysterious. They're seers! They have peered over the temporal walls of earthly existence and witnessed what awaits. They live this present life subconsciously.

If we're not careful we will become so desperate and hungry that we will swallow anything, regardless if it is fit for spiritual consumption.

They are difficult to entertain. Like Paul the apostle, they have ascended to heavenly dimensions and cannot find words to express the splendor (see 2 Cor. 12:2-4).

They may accumulate some assets but are not infatuated by them. Gehazi may be enamoured with the garments of Naaman, but Elisha is not (see 2 Kings 5:15-24). The mantle is not a fashion statement and at times has the weight of a cumbersome cross. It opens doors for one's ministry and causes many to be closed. But the old prophet will take it to his grave.

Bona fide Blessings

Heavy overhead can make it hard to be objective. The temptation exists to choose talent over morality. After all, it is imperative that we remain the biggest show in town. Competition's tough! And thus another nail is driven into the coffin containing our conscience.

A clarion call is being issued; take heed. If one listens, the tolling of the bells can be distinguished, summonsing intercessors to prayer. That which is spiritual is conceived in labor-intensive supplication. We need fewer planning sessions and more prayer meetings.

I am not interested in a revival that looks almost like the real thing. The precious anointing of the apothecary is too valuable to be sacrificed on the altar of convenience. If the Lord has to peel away, layer by layer, my self-sufficiency, may the process begin. If, as it was the case with Paul (see 2 Cor. 12:9), He chooses to perfect His strength through my weakness, I stand ready for the process to begin.

My soul yearns for fresh manna, a current word from God. I can't tolerate silence of the Spirit. I cannot be expected to survive on antiquated assertions. I refuse to rendezvous with a surrogate. I will prevail in His presence until the *promise* is conceived within my spirit.

I am not looking for a pinch-hitter to step up to the plate and do my bidding. There is no substitute for the original power of Pentecost. I will endure a sterile existence until the promise is conceived within my spirit.

The Premise for Power

I believe this partly answers the question of why God chose Abraham and Sarah and why it seemingly took so long. He has to bring us to that blessed place of weakness before He can manifest His strength. It is a spiritual formula. S (S= strength) + S = nothing; S + W (W= weakness) = fulfillment.

Weakness is an unpopular subject today. It is certainly not something that is viewed as an asset. There are various courses and workshops that assist in transforming your weaknesses into strengths. This is beneficial in the secular world but in some instances is an impediment in our spiritual life.

Self-sufficiency has robbed many of encountering El-Shaddai. We despise the idea of becoming weak. We cannot handle not being in complete control of our lives. We can offer numerous explanations as to why we must be in control: *My personality demands it. I am choleric, type A, passive aggressive. I am an alpha-male and I can't help my having to be in command. It is the hunter-gatherer mindset inbred in my psyche.*

We are fixated on security and cherish the warm, feathery interior of our cushy nests. We work hard getting all of our ducks in a row, and we don't need anything spoiling our program. *If it ain't broke, don't break it.* Every church and every Christian is susceptible to the addictive sedative known as contentment.

Ezekiel only discovered supernatural power when he went off the deep end. When he got in over his head, and there was no bridge to retreat, he encountered the depths of God's unfathomable ability (see Ezek. 47:1-5).

Heroes With Hang-ups

Another issue concerning our weaknesses is that we conceal and try to disguise them because we are inhibited by what other people will think. The very thing causing you to anguish and feel inadequate may be the impetus in God's blessing you.

Moses was not an eloquent emissary; Gideon—not exactly a gladiator; nor Leah—good looking, Rahab—chaste, Jacob—a role model, Caleb—a spring chicken, Elijah—mild-tempered, Solomon—monogamous, Amos—a city slicker, Zacchaeus—honest, Peter—loyal. The list could go on and on but you get the picture.

The deficiencies on this list can be found in quite diverse categories: physical attributes, charisma, oratory, and even spiritual and moral. This is not to make a case for sanctioning sin but to illustrate how being a paragon of perfection is not a prerequisite in being used of the Lord. Our frailties and flaws do not repel God; they attract Him to us.

Matthew and Mark have written a good example of this • in their Gospels. There was a man who possessed the intestinal fortitude to enter the synagogue even though he had a withered hand (see Mt. 12:10; Mk. 3:1). The crippled and deformed were not permitted to enter the temple. Jesus not only disclosed that such a convalescent was present, He asked him to reveal his infirmity. Jesus commanded him to stretch forth his arm.

In the house where God dwells *weakness* is not a bad word; it is the password. That's why the Pharisees were in His midst but not in His presence. They met the Galilean but never encountered the Glory. Their good deeds were insurmountable and obstructed their vision from receiving a revelation of deity.

When Jesus heard it, He saith unto them, They that are whole have no need of the physician, but they that are sick: I came not to call the righteous, but sinners to repentance (Mark 2:17).

And it came to pass on a certain day, as He was teaching, that there were Pharisees and doctors of the law sitting by, which were come out of every town of Galilee, and Judaea, and Jerusalem: and the power of the Lord was present to heal them (Luke 5:17).

Read the Scripture again. Who were in attendance? Pharisees and doctors of the law! "And the power of the Lord was present to heal them." Could it be that the presence of the Lord was there to heal self-righteousness, skepticism, and cynicism? My opinion is it takes nothing short of a miracle to cure such incredulity.

Habitat for Humanity

The church is not a museum of magnificence but a hospital for the hopeless. It is not a column-lined rotunda where the statuesque figures of Adonis, Zeus, and Hercules stand poised atop marble pedestals, flaunting superhuman strength. It is more of an infirmary where one admits his weakness and limps into the affectionate arms of mercy. It is a triage assembled anytime, anyplace, to render aid in times of crises.

It does not exemplify extravagant architecture and emit pleasant aromas. Things get messy and the air gets stinky due to the patients constantly being admitted. No one is refused care. No need to produce proof of insurance. Actuaries don't cover sin.

No one here has an "S" emblem on his or her T-shirt. Talent scouts may not be proposing multimillion-dollar contracts, but don't worry about making the draft. As one person said, "God doesn't need your ability, just your availability." You may have sprung from an inferior gene pool and been reared in a less than perfect environment. Perhaps every branch on your family tree could use a good pruning. Regardless of past rejections, here you'll find acceptance.

While the Pauline epistles advocate modesty and moderation in all things, at our best we remain fallible and fleshly: "That which is born of the flesh is flesh" (Jn. 3:6a). We can flex bulging biceps and boast of great achievements, but still fall painfully short of His holiness. Unless we rely completely on His strength, we can shout until we injure our vocal chords; but we will accomplish nothing more than benign prayers and anemic sermons.

The nativity of powerful ministries is not gothic cathedrals with looming spires. Many were plucked from the furnace of tribulation and hammered into shape on the anvil of adversity. All were dredged from the bottom of an ocean of iniquity, covered in filth, and shackled with sin. One of the greatest preachers who ever lived explained it most adequately: "But by the grace of God I am what I am" (1 Cor. 15:10a). A onetime persecutor of the Church became a propagator of the gospel.

What a wonder! Once drug addicts now preachers, prostitutes now daughters of Zion. Everyone here has a horrendous history, and because of marvelous grace, a favorable future. There are some whose pasts are much more checkered than others, some whose spiritual handicap is much more pronounced than others, but without exception all recognize His strength is perfected through our weakness. All at some time or another have met face-to-face with failure and would still be there had it not been for God's unconditional love.

Whether intellect or illiterate, Wall Street trader or welfare recipient; whether living in a posh downtown condo or a graffiti-scribbled overpass, God sees no difference. Whether you graduated from Harvard or were a gang-banger in Harlem, neither will impress nor impede here. The remarkable cleansing power of the blood of Jesus Christ ascends the loftiest elevation and plunges to the base of the deepest valley.

For ye see your calling, brethren, how that not many wise men after the flesh, not many mighty, not many noble, are called: but God hath chosen the foolish things of the world to confound the wise; and God hath chosen the weak things of the world to confound the things which are mighty; and base things of the world, and things which are despised, hath God chosen, yea, and things which are not, to bring to nought things that are: that no flesh should glory in His presence (1 Corinthians 1:26-29).

Achieving Weakness

God purposely puts us in the weakening process. This is extremely difficult for us to cope with. We become distressed as Sarah did and attempt to remedy the situation ourselves. We more or less try to help God out. As the evening shadows of our life begin to accumulate and grow more vivid we begin to panic. When our faith begins to waver and time is of the essence, we solicit Hagar to assist in conceiving our promise. The only thing this accomplishes is to delay the promise even longer. God will not place His endorsement on that which man has manufactured.

The natural mind with all of its astonishing aptitude and ingenuity cannot furnish a solution for that which is spiritual. The apostle Paul explained it is because the carnal mind is not subject to the law of God and neither indeed can be (see Rom. 8:7).

Sarah may have well been past the flower of her age but old Abe still had a spark of energy remaining. Ishmael was proof of that. When the old fellow finally reached the blessed place of weakness and no longer possessed the power to produce a son, the promise came to pass.

In order to achieve greatness you first must embrace weakness. Actually you don't have to be pretentious, everyone has a substantial amount. Some can't admit to any, and that itself is a weakness.

All who have encountered El-Shaddai claim the same alma mater: the academy of weakness. Somewhere along the pilgrimage they were liberated from fetters that constrained them to security and separated themselves from the status quo. They accepted the challenge and entrusted their fate to the hands of God.

When David was weak, he was powerful. As a lad he withstood Goliath, armed with a name and a sling, and gave Israel a new song to sing. Not a soldier or a brother accompanied him in the valley of Elah when he confronted the giant (see 1 Sam. 17:41-51). But, as he grew older he made the mistake of numbering Israel. His faith was not in God alone but in the 1.3 million valiant men of war (see 2 Sam. 24:9-10). His confidence in manpower caused him woe.

The key to highly effective ministers and leaders is they have an understanding of weakness. I have read testimonies from Charles Haddon Spurgeon to Bishop T.D. Jakes, in which they referred to this very process. The most outstanding spiritual leaders of our day will quickly tell you it is as much of a mystery to them as it is to us why God chose to use them in such a unique manner.

Hurry up and throw in the towel. Kneel at the feet of Christ and admit your incompetence. Say *uncle*, slap the mat, raise the white flag. Do whatever it takes to yield. Once you cross the threshold of weakness you enter the sphere of the supernatural. Recognizing your limitations is the segue to success.

When Isaac was born, I don't think Abraham stepped out of his tent, undid the top four buttons of his robe, inhaled deeply, and paraded around with his chest protruding. He was very much aware of God's involvement in this scenario. His contribution was of very little consequence.

God doesn't need me to preach, praise, or write. He lets me participate in these activities as worship. I am certain I amuse audiences and editors as I endeavor to articulate my thoughts, with my limited talent, through the mediums of writing and preaching. God welcomes it as an offering. A wordsmith can mesmerize the reader, but impressing God is somewhat different. It is not skillful sentence structuring and flawless grammar that please Christ. Rather, sincere expressions of affection from a grateful heart never fail to move God.

My most cherished memorabilia are notes and pictures my daughters gave to me when they were youngsters. I have a collection that ranges from homemade birthday cards to the BEST DAD IN THE WORLD award. Whenever I retrieve any of these paper treasures from my desk drawer I pause and my thoughts become suspended in the timeframe during which they were produced.

These are creations from unpretentious little girls who wanted to convey their love to Daddy. They succeeded. The artwork and spelling put a smile on my face and a lump in my throat. Their renditions wouldn't solicit high bids at a Sotheby's auction but are invaluable to me. I know they love their father, and these expressions on paper move me to tears.

It is midnight as I write this particular passage. I'm holed up in another hotel room feeling lonesome. Late in the evening is when constant traveling loses whatever glamor it may have possessed. Memories are coming out of storage bins in my mind. I recall the self-composed songs Datha and Kayla sang. Their tiny unsteady voices could belt out some interesting tunes. While the lyrics lacked rhyme, they possessed passion. It tickled me then and tears me up now. I think I have tapped into some of what God feels.

The Paradox of Power

No ministry has strength without the element of weakness. It is kind of a divine paradox. If Zacchaeus had been of normal stature he may not have discovered salvation. He was vertically challenged, yet he did not allow his genetic deficiency to dissuade him. He just climbed above it and went out on a limb (see Lk. 19:2-6). Had Gideon not been an undercover wheat thresher he may not have become a mighty man of valor. He was supposed to thresh wheat at the threshing floor, but he was doing it at a winepress, to hide it from the Midianites (see Judg. 6:11). The shortness of Zacchaeus and the cowardice of Gideon resulted in blessings.

Finding faults is not a discovery; God has been aware of them all the time. He calls the ones with flaws and frailties intentionally, not ignorantly. They're the ones who can be entrusted with victory without robbing the glory.

God is attracted to our weakness so don't hide it. The royal guards may snicker as you stutter and stammer; *La-lel-let mah-ma-my pa-p-p-p-p-people gah-go!* However, Pharoah's valiant army will be subdued because of the anointing. The story is told of a preacher who said to the Lord, "I'm just a two-by-four." The Lord replied, "You're a one-by-nothing. I'm the one and you're nothing." And without Him we truly are nothing.

Remaining Weak

Constant reliance on the Holy Spirit must always be maintained as you develop a gift and have remarkable confirmations accompany your ministry. Never make the mistake of placing your faith in your gift and the fruit of your ministry. You enter a dangerous place when all your passion is focused on the blessing and not the Blesser.

I think the possibility exists that Isaac began to slip into a chamber of Abraham's heart that was reserved only for God. Whenever he looked at the boy he saw the fulfillment and source of the promise. That may be what initiated the darkest and most sleepless night he would have to endure.

And He said, Take now thy son, thine only son Isaac, whom thou lovest, and get thee into the land of Moriah; and offer him there for a burnt offering upon one of the mountains which I will tell thee of (Genesis 22:2).

Try as I may, I cannot comprehend the anguish that Abraham must have gone through. I wonder if there wasn't a moment where he grabbed his chest in order to prevent his heart from leaping out. Sunrises remaining at that point in his life may have quite possibly been numbered in double digits. Perhaps he hoped it was a case of senility rather than God speaking to him.

At that juncture in his life the odds of having anything of this magnitude occur were stacked against him. He had lived beyond 100 years and it only happened once; how could it ever occur again? You just don't turn loose something this special so easily.

Can it be that we get so intoxicated on the anointing that we can't let it go? We've fallen in love with the gifts more than the Giver! Our ministries merit more of our attention and time than God does!

"You mean you want my boy, not my beast? You want my best, not my beast?" Abraham gladly would have sacrificed the premium member of his flock and for that matter all of his livestock. If silver and gold could have appeased Jehovah he would have bankrupted himself. Anything but Isaac!

Can it be that we get so intoxicated on the anointing that we can't let it go? We've fallen in love with the gifts more than the Giver! Our ministries merit more of our attention and time than God does! We experience such a degree of success that we begin to believe our own press reports! Ministries today can come fully loaded with a lot of perks and privileges that can make it extremely difficult to relinquish.

Or do we become complacent as we watch Isaac mature, rapidly moving toward manhood? Maybe this is what prompts God to yank our chain and remind us that He alone is our source of all things. Perhaps Abraham looked to Isaac as the origin, from whom the innumerable nation would proceed, and God was saying, "Look, I can do this with or without the boy."

Have we forgotten how completely unproductive we were before God intervened in our sterile existence? Is there a chance we rely on our silver-tongued oratory and captivating charisma rather than an unction from the Holy One? Perhaps protocol demands programs rather than prayer. Prayer and fasting is old school mentality. Just institute a new curriculum that has proven successful in some other church.

Was God playing mind games with Abraham when asking him to take his son to Moriah? Or was it just to provide typology for an event 4,000 years in the future? During that same era, heathens were sacrificing their children to Molech (see Lev. 18:21); perhaps God was testing Abraham to see if he possessed equal dedication to the one true God. A myriad more answers to the query have been provided over the years.

It is obvious that it was a test of some sort. Every advancement we make in the Kingdom is proceeded by a season of testing. Solomon's throne had six steps that led up to it with two stone lions on every step—one on the left and one on the right (see 1 Kings 10:20). With every step we take, we are tested on every side. As Francis Frangipane one time said, "New level new devil!"

Also, I think once again we encounter the value of weakness here at Moriah. I believe that God was extracting two words from Abraham's vocabulary: *my* and *mine*. He'll descend the mount with his boy, he'll hold him, touch him, and enjoy all the paternal rights that go with fatherhood. But he will be acutely aware that God produced him and can take him whenever He chooses. He'll walk very softly from here on out, making no great claims, and taking nothing for granted.

There may be a time when God will demand a great sacrifice on your part. It doesn't seem logical that He would call you, anoint you, use you, and then demand that you offer it all back to Him. God can divinely lead someone into business; it flourishes, an affluent lifestyle is enjoyed, and missionary efforts are blessed around the world as a result of their giving. Why would God then stretch His arm, unfold His fingers, and request it all back?

It is one of the greatest lessons in weakness you will ever be schooled in. It is an education far superior to what Yale and Harvard can provide. Seminary may have instructed you adequately in church history, doctrine, exegetical theology, and perhaps you are a master at hermeneutics. However, this really is the one subject they don't teach you in business classes at Harvard, or in ministry seminars at Bible college.

It can be learned only in practical terms, not in theory. When you not only have *seen that mountain* but have stood on its peak; when you have witnessed the realization of your dreams and have watched them flourish before you, only to see God pluck them from your life; it is like watching a gardener snip life-filled flowers from a garden. You remember the beautiful fragrance each blossom afforded your senses, but presently only stems remain. Not even a hint of the pleasant aroma or a trace of the velvety, pastel colors painted on their delicate petals lingers.

It appears that you'll never experience success again. The company is now just a silent structure, not a burgeoning business. The marriage is void of intimacy and affection, and life with your mate has become subsistence—a far cry from the invigorating passion that it once possessed. The fantasy has been removed from your dream and a ghastly figure enters the scene, turning it into a horrific nightmare.

Nostalgia clinches your emotions as you reminisce of a bygone day when you walked onto the rostrum, stepped into the pulpit, and under the canopy of divine anointing. The flame has been reduced to a flicker, threatening to extinguish. You do not share the sentiments of the weeping prophet Jeremiah, who characterized it as "fire shut up in his bones" (see Jer. 20:9).

Instead of warmth the air is frigid, a harbinger of spiritual insolvency. It appears as though the winter season has entered your life for good. It would be so much easier to endure if you weren't tormented with pictures from the past. They lie concealed in infinitesimal memory cells, but emerge from dormancy with enormous impact. For moments at a time your mind is arrested by the thoughts of a once-thriving ministry.

God has no intention of not returning your promise. But when Isaac climbs down from the hard stones of the altar and steps back into your arms and your life, you will acquire a reverence you have never had. Now your comprehension of weakness has been enlightened.

The business ascends from the ashes like the fabled Phoenix, breaking every previous record. Divorce statistics are minus another shattered marriage as you and yours turn over a new leaf and begin anew.

The gentle breeze of the Holy Spirit ruffles a few stray hairs on the top of your head as a rhemah stirs deep within your spirit. At one time you were resigned to never minister again. But after that memorable mountaintop experience, you enter a dimension you have never experienced. Everyone in attendance sits in awe, beholding the fresh anointing.

Go ahead, love the lad and call him son. Assume the position of patriarch. At times the outcome was questionable but you persevered and passed the test. Your weakness has proven to be your strength. It was a long and lonely journey but you finally arrived. Go on, get on home and raise *your* son. Keep the promise in perspective.

Chapter Three

THE ODD COUPLE

*The Spirit itself beareth witness with our spirit, that we are the children of God: and if children, then heirs; heirs of God, and joint-heirs with Christ; if so be that we suffer with **Him**, that we may be also glorified together. For I reckon that the sufferings of this present time **are** not worthy to **be compared** with the glory which shall be revealed in us* (Romans 8:16-18, emphasis added).

Some people never seem to mature. They grow old but somehow fail to grow up. It is one thing to be a senior with a sense of humor, quite another to be one acting out inane antics. I have some wonderful acquaintances who have been members of the AARP for several years and are always a joy to be around. They joke about everything from my quickly ascending the aging ladder to their own physical decadence. Pining away their remaining days is not their thing; instead they have opted to enjoy every moment of life.

One would think that someone well into his or her 70s would be far beyond pulling pranks—not innocent pranks, but the kind that can have lifetime consequences! Not so with Jacob. He was in his mid- to upper-70s when he fraudulently acquired his brother Esau's birthright.*

It's apparent he was not wet behind the ears—certainly not a novice at deception, but a conniver to the core. Clearly, guile was in his genes. Although a twin, Jacob was a few moments younger than Esau. But when Jacob exited his mother's womb he had hold of Esau's heel. It appears as though he plotted to trip up his brother from the womb (see Gen. 25:26).

His misdeed sent him packing and impelled him from his home. Jacob repeatedly practiced this pattern of deception, targeting those who were unaware of his reputation. Everything Jacob possessed was by ill-gotten means. For some time

She is not adorned in elegant garments, dancing gracefully across the polished ballroom floor. She is on her way to water livestock and wearing ordinary apparel.

---

* In Genesis 41:46-54 Joseph was 30 years old when he stood before Pharaoh at the beginning of the seven plenteous years. After those years and two more years of famine, when Joseph was 39, his brothers, their families, and their father Jacob, came down to be with him in Egypt. Jacob was 130 years old at this point (see Gen. 47:9). This means that Jacob was 91 years old when Joseph was born in Haran. It was then that Jacob wanted to return from Haran to his own people in Canaan but Laban persuaded him to remain six more years (see Gen. 30:25-28, 31:38-41). The stay in Haran was 20 years of which six were spent after Joseph's birth, and then we know that Joseph was born in the 14th year of Jacob in Haran. Counting back 14 years from his age of 91 at Joseph's birth we thus find him about 77 when he first came to Haran looking for a wife.

he lived on the lam; a vagabond, always being cognizant of his past, wondering when the odds were going to catch up with him.

The snapshot we now see of Jacob is the wanderer standing in a field, beholding a drop-dead gorgeous woman approach with her silky locks undulating in the gentle breeze. She is not adorned in elegant garments, dancing gracefully across the polished ballroom floor. She is on her way to water livestock and wearing ordinary apparel. However, the backdrop does not diminish her ravishing looks.

It's a textbook case of love at first sight. Her name is Rachel. In Jacob's defense, he probably didn't stand a chance; she was a real heartthrob. There probably wouldn't be any member of the male gender not attracted to such incredible beauty (see Gen. 29:17).

Jacob is every dad's nightmare. Knowing that full well I am raising children for someone else, I can only hope and pray the young men in my daughters' lives will possess better pedigrees than that of Jacob's.

Maybe, by the time suitors come calling, there will be an instant background check in place to evaluate their character. Nothing very comprehensive, just enough information to substantiate financial status, DNA analysis, and any criminal history.

What a scoundrel! He kisses Rachel *before* the first date (see Gen. 29:11)! That tells me he is not the kind of man I want my daughters getting tangled up with. The *what's-in-it-for-me* kind: They dote on your daughters but you know full well they are full of ulterior motives.

They have perfected all the moves and well-rehearsed lines that have a way of wooing and luring the most informed.

Like sequoias that have survived hurricane gales, ferocious tornadoes, and desert-like drought, but are leveled by chainsaws, young ladies fall prey to these debonair male predators.

Surely Jacob has one more conspiracy in the back of his cranium that will secure a relationship with this fair damsel. He is sharp and has the ability to think on his feet. His brain shifts into overdrive and the strategizing begins. Jacob ingeniously begins to spin a web and Rachel is about to be caught in his masterful scheme. *Oh, what a tangled web we weave...*

Laban, Rachel's dad, approaches Jacob and offers him gainful employment on his farm (see Gen. 29:15). However, Laban is nobody's fool. He has met this kind before. Most likely Jacob was hired to do chores the other farmhands shied away from.

Dear Ole Dads

Fathers have a built-in sophisticated radar system that can spot scalawags a mile away. A microscopic blip registers visibly on the screen. Mothers often get swept off their feet by their charm. Dads remain poised and unaffected by their superficiality.

Interviewing applicants for employment is one thing; evaluating future son-in-laws is quite another. The worker can always be terminated; the son-in-law may have to he tolerated. I recently was told how one dad handled an uncomfortable situation. When a young man asked for his daughter's hand in marriage, he replied, "I just bought a shotgun, and I don't even hunt."

When Jacob feels confident that he has dispelled any negative feelings Laban may have had of him, he approaches

Laban and begins to worm his way in the corridors of his heart. With the dexterity of an artist and resolve of an Olympian, he attempts his quest for the gold.

Previously, his subtlety has afforded him a considerable measure of success. If he can pull this off it will make acquiring the birthright look like a walk in the park. If he can camouflage his questionable character and summons his best behavior, he will relish in the triumph of his greatest conquest.

Love does that to you. The affection within burns with such intensity it nullifies any multiplicity and creates a singularity. Minds that experience rampant thoughts, like congested urban expressways at five o'clock on Friday evening, are subdued and can only think of one thing. College careers, parental advice, and common sense all lose to love. Sacrifices that must be made to accommodate these incredulous relationships are justified with the ideology of *living on love.*

The High Cost of Love

The criterion Laban requires is not easy to provide. In order for Jacob to win the hand of Rachel, he will have to labor seven years (see Gen. 29:18). Seven years! Seven years of toiling amid muck, mire, tramping through pastures laden with dung, working one's fingers to the bones is no easy task.

The stakes are high, the ante is expensive, but Rachel is beautiful. The young lady must have been charming. Jacob places the dowry and Rachel in the counterbalance and Rachel wins. Aching back, sweating brow, callused hands, and severely inflamed sinuses are not enough to dissuade Jacob. Day after day, from dawn to dusk he clocks in for work.

Seven long, arduous years seemed but a few days (see Gen. 29:20). Sounds quite possibly like the worse case of lovesickness ever recorded. The annals of history corroborate how powerful men can become incompetent to the seductive overtures of the female species. Laying siege to cities, overthrowing monarchies, and conquering kingdoms are one thing; man's attraction to women, another.

Fatal Attraction

More than likely you've read the book or watched the movie of the alluring Egyptian queen. Whether it was Cleopatra's enchanting singing voice, ability to speak nine languages, or political savvy that arrested the attention of Mark Antony is anyone's guess. The coins upon which her face is inscribed most certainly do not suggest beauty, but rather masculine characteristics. When he summoned the ostentatious queen of Egypt to Tarsus, Cleopatra put on a spectacular show. She arrived on a barge with gilded stern, purple sails, and silver oars, flanked by maids dressed as sea nymphs, and boys dressed like Cupid. Cleopatra masqueraded as Venus, goddess of love.

One night with Cleopatra proved to be sufficient to apprehend Antony's heart and lock it in a grip that he would never be able to break. Their relationship which spanned several years was filled with deceit and betrayal, yet Antony could not stay away. After hearing the news that Cleopatra was dead, Mark Antony ordered his servant, Eros, to slay him. Eros killed himself. Antony thanked the servant for showing his master how to perform the task he didn't have the heart to carry out, and then plunged the knife into his own stomach.

Upon finding Antony, servants carried his wounded body to Cleopatra's mausoleum, who was not dead after all. Mark Antony died in her arms. This is an eerie example of the cement-like hold love can attain. If you linger too long, the mortar sets; you are anchored for good.

A Lesson in Love

Never had a sunrise given birth to such a splendid day. Proud of the fact he completed his tenure, Jacob anxiously awaits his reward. Some things are worth waiting for, some worth fighting for, and some worth dying for. To Jacob, Rachel is worthy of all the above. The courtship is complete. Tonight they will become one. They will consummate their marriage after seven years of abstinence.

I am deeply curious of the weather conditions in the Middle-Eastern sky that fateful night. Perhaps clouds eclipsed the moon and stars were obstructed from emitting their soft, glittering light. Maybe there was just enough breeze to extinguish candles and torches. There must have been a lighting problem.

The morning after the honeymoon the new bride is awakened by the worst sound she could ever imagine hearing, *aaaaaaahhhhhhhhhh*! This doesn't sound anything like Eureka! A blacksmith's bellows never discharged more exhalation. Houston! We have a problem!

It's not Rachel. I repeat, it is not Rachel in Jacob's tent. It is her older sister, Leah (see Gen. 29:25). I am sure many surprises have occurred on wedding nights; this however, probably wins hands down. Although it might not be a bad scenario in some cases, this morning it is the worst possible one. Leah is *tender eyed* (see Gen. 29:17).

Speculation exists over the definition of *tender eyed*. I think I have a viable interpretation. Leah has a face only a father can love. It is undeniable that some do not possess facial attributes that are becoming. When Mother Nature distributed good looks, she somehow bypassed Leah.

Possibly, a new flap was created in the tent as Jacob grabbed his robe and, heart pounding in absolute terror, fled the scene. Scripture does not record whether Jacob asked if she could sing. It is one thing to be shortchanged, quite another to be swindled. This is not an innocent oversight, but a conspiracy, involving lifetime consequences.

Leah is not an evil temptress that would cause you to squander marital bliss. You're not going to pack up and pull out to begin a new life, leaving behind a healthy home. Wives don't become paranoid when Leah is present. Not many husbands have been busted for gaping at her.

Ante Up!

The cows have come home. Deception has produced a bitter harvest. Jacob's dilemma has every appearance of a clandestine plan by Laban, or is it? If it is a lie, perhaps an annulment can be arranged. If it is a law, however, he is going to have to face reality and learn to live with it.

> *And Laban said, It must not be so done in our country, to give the younger before the firstborn. Fulfill her week, and we will give thee this also for the service which thou shalt serve with me yet seven other years* (Genesis 29:26-27).

Reality has dawned in Jacob's life. He has successfully circumvented issues and evaded obstacles in the past. The time has come to exercise integrity or revert to old ways and escape. According to the law of the land, correct wages have been awarded for services rendered.

Jacob should have read the fine print at the bottom of the page before he endorsed the contract. Rachel is not removed from the equation. There are contingencies that must be met in order for the marriage to materialize. Some may opine it is a case of poetic justice.

The concessions include learning to love something he despises, embracing someone he prefers not to touch, and living with something he dislikes.

Reality Check

Jacob needs to put everything into perspective. Leah may have an unattractive face, but Jacob has an ugly heart. He is the antithesis of an honest man. Leah's face is understandable; Jacob's fraud is unquestionable. Leah can't change the fact she is older than Rachel and less desirable.

This drama has more to do with destiny than deceit. Jacob has been nominated for notoriety. Future generations will include his name along with others who are worthy of honor. Echoing throughout the centuries will be the names Abraham, Isaac, and Jacob. He can ascend and sit alongside dignity if he can adhere to the tenets of equity.

Jacob thinks he has a clear comprehension of what love is all about. What he doesn't know is, Leah has been led into his life to illuminate his understanding. Presently, love is a pretty face packaged with a trim physique whose name is Rachel. But a lady named Leah will become his tutor and through this alliance he will come to appreciate humility.

When you laid eyes on Christ, it was love at first sight. What wasn't there to love? When He shifted His compassionate eyes in your direction, you looked into the face of God. A holy hunger was kindled in your heart and you knew that right away it would ignite your entire being. You became consumed with Him.

Every waking moment thoughts of Jesus dominated your mind. As your head rested on the pillow you meditated on His everlasting Word. You discovered the Lover of your soul. Whatever you had to lay down or pick up, hold onto or let go of, you agreed wholeheartedly. Love does that to you.

This romance with Royalty permeated the veneer of temporal interests. The earthly lost its appeal and Heaven gained your affection. You took advantage of every opportunity to be in His presence. The time passed quickly and you loathed the idea of leaving this sanctuary of unimpaired serenity.

Any potential you possessed was volunteered unconditionally. Whether the field was foreign or domestic did not matter. His indwelling Spirit compelled you to proclaim of love so infinite that it encompassed all of space and could rescue the vilest of sinners.

The decision you made had every intention of being a long-term commitment. Reneging on your covenant was not a prenuptial insurance policy where you could contest on grounds of dissatisfaction.

Then one morning in your newfound relationship you awaken alongside of something that isn't beautiful. The face of ugliness is lying next to you. Something has gone horribly wrong. It appears as though useless weeds have invaded your tranquil, botanical garden. The rose whose magnificent fragrance exhilarated your senses wounds you with its barbed thorns.

You weren't exactly anticipating tiptoeing through the tulips, but this is inconceivable. Christians are not expected to coexist with anything this offensive. You may not be the reddest apple on the tree; however, you feel worthy of something a little more compatible.

Be careful when you point your index finger in the face of the Almighty and accuse Him of not being fair. Instead, thank Him for not being fair—He's fantastic! If God gave us what we did deserve, we'd be dead. Instead, He gave us what we do not deserve, everlasting life.

In spite of trials we presently may be experiencing, we all are faring much better than we deserve. Living for God is not such a bad thing! Besides, everything we have to give up to go to Heaven, we have to give up to go to hell! It just makes so much better sense to lay vices aside, and endure what many times are simply life's hardships, and go to Heaven.

The victim mentality will fasten to your spirit like barnacles clinging to the bow of a boat. It requires an adroit ear and keen eye to detect its stealthy approach. It lavishes sympathy on your emotions and justifies any thought of malice. As a matter of fact, it solicits you into the arena of animosity to seek retribution.

Your unpleasant circumstance is not an anomaly. God is not mistreating you by obligating you to tribulations no one else can bear. If you continue to entertain feelings of self-pity you will submerse yourself into an abyss of despair you may not be able to be retrieved from.

Any way we look at it, God did not stumble onto a bargain when He redeemed humanity. I guess that explains the adjective used to describe grace—*amazing*. Break *amaze* into its two syllables: *a-maze*. It's a maze! I cannot comprehend such unmerited favor. It is a puzzle that exhausts my ingenuity and enthralls me with absolute wonderment. The ramifications are incalculable, the reach immeasurable, the depth unfathomable, and the rationale inexplicable.

Who Do You Love?

There are some things from which we all would like to separate. Personally, I have never placed the welcome mat out for financial woes, disharmony in the home, or physical maladies. I certainly have never wanted to develop a relationship with trials and tribulation. My impulse would be to evict them immediately if they took up residence in my life.

There is a divine order of events, which God has engineered, that renders His glory and envelops us with anointing. Often they go against the grain of our flesh and provoke us to pray for their removal. We study the landscape to see if there is an alternative route to skirt these hazards and still arrive at our destiny. Sooner or later we resign to embark on the journey and accept His will, or linger forever to wonder what might have been.

What attracts us to church and to ministry? Do we have an appetite for the fruit of the Spirit or are we infatuated over the gifts of the Spirit? Perhaps, to some, the church has become the safest financial institution to invest in. The returns are fantastic and the risk, minimal. With a credible name like *Jesus*, and collateral like golden streets for security, one can hardly go wrong.

The health plan is adequate. With miracles and healing available, suffering is not expected. Social acceptance? The consensus couldn't be better. Modern crosses don't seem to be as cumbersome as former ones. They really don't restrict us from associations and activities. Our own conscience is considered to be our guide. In an era when morality is plummeting and iniquity rising, this poses a dangerous threat.

If your church is not hip and does not participate in current trends, you can search the yellow pages or tune in to a commercial and find one that's more accommodating to your carnality. Don't make a hasty decision. Be sure to ascertain whether or not it is considered to be the prominent church in town. That way your attire will receive proper appreciation. Thank goodness for people who understand class. Sure makes it comfortable not having to share a pew with undesirables. Some churches have all the amenities of an exclusive club with the exception of having to produce a membership ID at the door. Sign up and join the fraternity.

Liberal contributions will not go unnoticed here. The right amount will inscribe your name larger than life on the new edifice. Philanthropy can reciprocate a handsome reward.

You will succeed in securing due recognition to your good name for generations to come: guaranteed homage to posterity.

Parishioners never grit their teeth and shake their head in disgust in response to demonstrative worship. The highest level of dignity is maintained at every gathering. Each segment of the service is tailored and choreographed right down to the tiniest detail. You may not encounter God but you will rub shoulders with an elite class of people.

Sin is nothing to get upset over. So what if you become a little covetous and find yourself living with your neighbor's wife. There's really no need to kneel at the altar and repent; go lay on the couch and be analyzed. Contrition is not necessary if you have a competent counselor.

If the Shekinah glory fails to descend, a display of pyrotechnics will grab the people's attention. No need to stay pent up in an office and immerse oneself in the Word. Crank up the computer and log on to a sermon site. They're a dime a dozen and the saints will never know the difference. Should attendance begin to wane, bite the bullet and write the check for a popular speaker. There are plenty with celebrity-like status guaranteed to be drawing cards.

If the demographics of a city are not idyllic, select another location to plant a church. It really isn't about conscientiously doing the will of God. The higher echelon of society will be a substantial contributor to your endeavor. Be sure to choose a neighborhood with the proper racial profile, one that is equivalent to your family.

You need not worry over lack of power if you have sufficient personality. The first is attained through fasting, the latter through feasting. Mingle with the right crowds, slap the right backs, and learn to play the game. Ecumenism is vogue; isolation isn't. Why fly solo. After all, doctrine only divides. Contemporary hermeneutics has pitched a big tent. Why stay outside?

Attend all the conferences, tee-off on the right courses, support the right causes, and before long you'll be invited into the inner circle. Update your wardrobe, upgrade your auto, dive into debt. Initiation was a hurdle, but you're finally through with the hassle. Anonymity inhibits you no longer. Accrue interest, enjoy friends, and ignore conviction. Explain to your family that it's a worthwhile investment. Live under the erroneous presumption that affluence is a panacea for all ills.

The Power of Love

If you remain captivated by Rachel, linger to reach out and take the hand of Leah. Desire can defeat disdain. Love will beckon to grace and form a coalition, providing strength to live with things you despise. The proving ground will become a launching pad and propel you to greatness.

Wrap your arms around Leah and draw her close; she is sent to be your savior from self-destruction. She brings balance, not beauty. Humility and anointing must consolidate and become constant companions. While one offers authority, the other offers stability.

Leah's face is ordinary: no distinguishing cheekbones; her smile is not irresistible. Her stride does not boast of self-confidence. She is unassuming, and would love to be gregarious, but finds it extremely difficult in the shadow of Rachel.

Your first impression is to flee, but give her a second thought. Humble pie is an acquired taste. Relax; you certainly won't choke to death, and it may even grow on you. Don't exaggerate your entitlements and underestimate Leah's attributes. Her unpretentious appearance is her redeeming virtue.

In your quest to procure what's right, you may forfeit what's best. Your heart has concluded there is no physical attraction and categorically denies any chemistry. You ardently attempt to convince God this relationship suffers from an absence of merit—a dichotomy destined for disaster. Negotiating is a futile attempt and will fail to convert God to concur with your sentiments.

Cleave to the lowly Nazarene in complete abandon. Stoke the dying embers of your being into the furnace of God's passion. Display a *do not disturb* sign on the door of your prayer chamber. Barricade your flesh inside until the winds of the Spirit breathe upon your soul, resuscitating your fervency.

Emancipate your ministry from vanity and dismiss the dictates of your ego. Recapture the disposition of meekness that contemptuous humanity has robbed from your ministry. Scrutinize each motive under the most discriminating microscope to discern its authenticity. Submit every proposal and aspiration to Christ to see if they meet His approval.

Realize once again that tangible, temporal possessions will not follow us into the afterlife. Every minute detail in Heaven has been covered. Your mansion will be of such grandeur that you will not be able to enhance the décor in the least.

Don't be intimidated in shedding expensive raiment that camouflages insecurities and advertises success, in order to clothe yourself in sackcloth and ashes. The natural man will wail in disparagement as you deny him gratification. Periodic sessions of praying and fasting are essential in reminding the *old man* that he has been crucified with Christ. Seek for the endorsement of Heaven that transcends the sometimes disingenuous affirmation of peers.

The Height and Breadth of Christianity

Have you ever wanted someone to take Christianity and break it down to its lowest common denominator, eliminate the seminary terminology, and get to the bottom line? Jesus did exactly this when asked by the lawyer, "Which is the great commandment?" (Mt. 22:36)

Obviously this was a pharisaical professor of Old Testament law patronizing a humble carpenter. In His answer, Jesus encompassed the entirety of what living for God is all about. He equated the vertical and horizontal dimensions and communicated them in language a child could understand.

We get so involved with constructing cathedrals and developing denominations that we forget that these are just scaffolding.

> *Then one of them, which was a lawyer, asked Him a question, tempting Him, and saying, Master, which is the great commandment in the law? Jesus said unto him, Thou shalt love the Lord thy God with all thy heart, and with all thy soul, and with all thy mind. This is the first and great commandment. And the second is like unto it, Thou shalt love thy neighbour*

*as thyself. On these two commandments hang all the
law and the prophets* (Matthew 22:35-40).

Every now and then it does all of us good to revisit the
fundamentals, the building blocks, to what living for God is all
about. We get so involved with constructing cathedrals and developing denominations that we forget that these are just scaffolding. When the Church is presented to Christ as a chaste
virgin, we will behold Her beauty, not the temporary appara-
tus used in the construction.

Defining Humility

I want to caution against confusing authority with arro-
gance. Just because some people minister assertively does
not mean they are self-absorbed. Take note that if people are
ministering under a heavy anointing they have paid the price.
Somewhere in the past they were introduced to a lady named
Leah. And the reason they are greatly used of the Holy Spirit
is because they didn't reject her but instead embraced her.

When the pay was insufficient and the accommodations
were inadequate, they remained faithful to their calling. Their
steadfast allegiance caused them to survive one hardship after
another.

On the same theme let me say that humility is not about
wearing shoes without soles, and britches without creases. The
decision to buy an American car versus a European car is
made based on personal preference. I am not opposed to being
a good steward and paying for quality. If one's ministry requires him or her to travel on a corporate jet, so be it. Many

times ministries experience massive expansion and churches grow exponentially, which may require innovation.

I believe a good definition of humility is to always remain under authority. This is the very thing that gave lucifer, the onetime archangel, trouble. He decided he would ascend above the stars and be like the Most High, which caused him to be banished from Heaven. This should serve as a good example of the importance of submission.

> *For promotion cometh neither from the east, nor from the west, nor from the south. But God is the judge: He putteth down one, and setteth up another* (Psalm 75:6-7).

The Virus Called Self

Narcissism has spread from the secular world into mainstream religious circles. Its sinister objective is to substitute the unadulterated, infallible Word of God with politically correct lectures. It is attempting to reduce prophets to puppets and sanctity to sacrilege. It will invite you to the bargaining table and try to negotiate a deal for your dedication. It will offer larger crowds, prestigious pulpits, and your name posted on the brightest marquis.

This is not to suggest that ministering to millions is a diabolical scheme of satan. God may have predestined you to reach multitudes. Nor is it an attempt to slam the topic of prosperity. However, one must always keep in mind that the welfare of the soul is of much greater importance than materialism. Remember, to whom much is given much is required. Cynics don't take potshots at buzzards. They're staring down the gun barrel at eagles. Satan has never assembled his cabinet in an emergency summit to discuss the apathetic.

Power comes in a package. Each of the contents has been deliberately included to ensure optimum performance and safe operation. We like to discard some of the components that we deem useless. However, the negative element is as indispensable as the positive. I am apprehensive of people who cavort with Rachel but will not so much as acknowledge Leah. In my opinion, they have a defective wiring system and eventually will short-circuit.

They may ascend to lofty heights and soar amid azure skies, but eventually they will sputter and spiral downward. A conceited heart and inflated ego are kamikaze cabin crew, and experts in terrorist tactics. They will commandeer the flight and purposely navigate into a fatal thunderhead, imperiling the lives of everyone on board.

A man's pride shall bring him low: but honour shall uphold the humble in spirit (Proverbs 29:23).

Pride goeth before destruction, and an haughty spirit before a fall (Proverbs 16:18).

Lucifer, embittered because of his own acquiescing to pride, uses the same weapon on the saints. Reluctantly remembering how susceptible he became, even while living in uncontaminated surroundings, he is convinced that mortals, existing in an acutely corrupt environment, are much more vulnerable. This, in tandem with his opinion of being far superior to the measly human race, most likely accounts for his abhorrence of mankind. Thus pride is probably his weapon of choice.

Pride has a long line of descendants. Prayerlessness and humanism are part of the lineage. When a person is too arrogant to pray he or she becomes self-sufficient, and feels no need to consult with Heaven. The person whose heart once pulsated with the purpose of pleasing God becomes more focused on professionalism.

Myriad excuses immediately come rushing to our defense to justify our lack of prayer. If we truly were convinced that communicating with God was an absolute necessity, we wouldn't feel such indifference toward prayer.

Bona fide humility has been taken hostage and is rarely permitted to make an appearance of late. Competition is an accomplice, aided and abetted by affluence and acceptance. An imposter, *manufactured modesty*, has been broadly recognized as the genuine article. This is immensely pleasing to satan due to his counterfeiting strategy.

This clever impersonation not only lacks legitimacy, it negates the presence of God. The Holy Spirit is not impressed with flamboyancy or the other extreme, superficial humility, but is drawn to tenderheartedness. Contrition may not receive a warm reception in some of today's ecclesiastical constituencies, but Heaven places tremendous value on it.

The Lord is nigh unto them that are of a broken heart; and saveth such as be of a contrite spirit (Psalm 34:18).

Though the Lord be high, yet hath He respect unto the lowly: but the proud He knoweth afar off (Psalm 138:6).

The Kingdom of God has suffered terrible reproach due to alter egos. It's called playing the game, the Jekyl and Hyde syndrome. What people on the outside view is diametrically opposite to what people perceive on the inside. Not only will *you* become disillusioned as you question who's real and what's real, so will many whom you have influenced.

A minister friend of mine found himself in the hospital with severe symptoms, but no clear diagnosis or prognosis. While there he encountered a life-changing experience. It occurred one night as he lay trying to catch some sleep. A demonic spirit entered his room, approached his bed, and began to communicate with him. The evil presence paraded ministerial acquaintances that had fallen from grace across the screen of his mind. The demon asserted that my friend was no different and would succumb to seduction and temptation as well.

The next night he lay hoping not to have a repeat of the previous night when Jesus entered the hospital room. The atmosphere was opposite to the night before. Instead of the eerie, fear inducing atmosphere, a peace settled over him like a warm blanket. In just two words, Jesus assured him how never to fail. He said, "Be real."

Perhaps somewhere along the way you lost your footing, and your ministry no longer reflects any semblance of the high calling in Christ Jesus, but has been swept into the swift current of secularism. Grab onto the lifeline of righteousness and be spared from evolving into spiritual schizophrenia.

It may be that the calamity is intended to be the catalyst in protecting you from complacency. Any man would beam with pride to be seen in public with Rachel; so it is with the anointing. It has a magnetic attraction that amasses crowds who in turn have a tendency to place you on a pedestal. Life's trials keep you connected with reality so you won't take yourself too seriously.

The Pediatrics of Praise

Judah did not originate from Jacob's relationship with Rachel. Jacob is the daddy, but Leah is the mother (see Gen. 29:35). This uncomfortable union gave birth to praise. The family tree of Christ sprang from the same soil. The Branch, the Offspring, the Lion of the tribe of Judah basically began when Jacob embraced a lady named Leah.

Praise is not always conceived in matches made in Heaven. It is often birthed amid sorrow and enters the world from the loins of disappointment and despair. Examine the DNA of praise and it will be proven conclusively that Leah is the momma.

Praise is not the result of a scientific experiment nor is it incubated in the womb of a surrogate mother. Cloning may produce a shout and sound identical to worship; however, if you are going to have the authentic and attract the attention of the Almighty, don't be surprised if you experience some heartache.

As the Ark of the Covenant was returning to Israel, David danced demonstratively before it and every six steps offered animal sacrifices to the Lord—not a pleasant mental image.

Blood, entrails, and animal carcasses were heaped along the edges of the road (see 2 Sam. 6:13).

The highway of praise is not a scenic route with breathtaking views that capture the imagination of a photographer and allure pleasure-seeking vacationers. Road rage will never be encountered. The repulsive sight and stench of viscera explain the lack of traffic.

It does not take ideal acoustics evenly reflecting each octave and instruments played by virtuosos to usher in God's presence. It is the anointing resting on the singers, musicians, and worshipers as they unite in a concert of praise. Prayer and perseverance have elevated them into a dimension of worship that solicits the manifest presence of God.

Your attorney may call, your accountant beep in, both conveying bad news. Your marriage is ending, the audit just beginning. The tests say terminal, recovery seems doubtful, your nerves are coming unraveled. Your entire world shows symptoms of atrophy. You close your eyes, let out a sigh, and wonder how much you can tolerate.

Tempestuous billows pitch your vessel, threatening to plunge it to the floor of the ocean. Your future has never felt so frail. Eventually, the gale ceases, the sea regains its composure, and you survive another skirmish with the enemy.

Although times have been tough, the crisis fails to abort the work of the Holy Spirit. The problem comes with a purpose. That's why God lifts the hedge and permits it to touch, but not take, your life. The *hallelujah* that emerges from the innermost recess of your throbbing heart warrants an audience with the

King. He who is continuously surrounded with talent that is out of this world becomes entranced with the fruit of your lips.

An interlude is initiated in Glory as the cherubic choir becomes engrossed with your singing. The ballad is self-composed, not with illustrious lyrics and melodious tunes, but with exceeding gratitude to God for His faithfulness. You are not a diva executing an aria from the renowned stage of La Scala, but a humble heart offering adoration to His Majesty.

The Geriatrics of Praise

Bethel was undoubtedly a milestone in Jacob's life. It was there that the prankster became a prince (see Gen. 32:28). The supplanter sired the sustainer (see Gen. 30:22-24), preserving the seed of Abraham. Not only did Jacob become Israel, but also Luz became Bethel (see Gen. 28:19). Change begets change. Change a man, change a home, change a city, change a nation, and change the world.

I am of the opinion that life with Leah brought about a metamorphosis. It may not be sound theology, but I think Jacob may have fallen in love with Leah. He eventually came to appreciate the qualities he failed to notice when they first met.

As he was arranging his own funeral and setting his affairs in order, he gave specific instructions concerning where he was to be buried. He distinctly commanded next to Leah (see Gen. 49:29-31). He not only became acquainted with meekness and humility, he also sustained a relationship and perhaps even a friendship to the very end.

Some encounters with grief and experiences with hardship will abide with us throughout this life. Petitioning God will not remove them and threatening to forgo the journey will not sway Him. God has selected them to travel with us, and insure we safely make it home. Along with goodness and mercy come meekness and humility. While some discourage us from going down and out, the other deters us from going up and out.

As time goes on, your attitude toward life's trials undergoes a change. Maturity eliminates the concern over what your contemporaries think of your living with Leah. You realize this is the way it is meant to be. You no longer argue or complain. You stop looking for excuses to leave.

You have attended school and learned how to handle blessings and burdens. Whether God decides to abound or abase you is not an issue. Those peering in from the peripheral may not view you a success. It has little to no effect on you. An inward contentment keeps your emotions in check.

The apostle Paul fervently prayed on three occasions that the thorn would be removed from his flesh. Finally, he received his answer. His ministry, anointing, and missionary journeys were not mentioned. The reply was all about grace (see 2 Cor. 12:7-9).

God's grace escapes the limitations of language and lexicon, and eclipses the most grievous situation. Grace can descend the staircase of a filthy Roman dungeon, stroll past poisonous vermin and disgusting feces, and comfort the lonely apostle who sits in solitary.

God does not expect us to live with something we cannot endure. He does not require us to carry something we cannot handle. Should God permit hardship access into our lives, He will also make sure sufficient grace is present.

Life is not just about suffering, trials, and tribulations. Think back to the gloomiest time in your life. There are probably plenty to choose from, more than you care to remember. Funeral homes, emergency rooms, prison cells, divorce courts. You likely have been to one; perhaps you've entered them all.

If the gloom was that gloomy, the glory will be glorious. The deepest, darkest, most deplorable misery you have experienced does not deserve to be written in the same category or placed on the same shelf as future glory.

Yesterday may have been disastrous, and today discouraging, but just keep looking ahead: Tomorrow is spectacular. You are a revelation waiting to be unveiled, an exquisite piece of artwork about to be exhibited. The celestial council will marvel at your brilliance and listen intently to your recount of grace.

The multicolored threads from the various experiences in your life were meticulously woven into a regal tapestry. The unattractive bride became a cherished companion. The uninvited anguish became an invaluable asset. The repulsive is partly responsible for your redemption. What you considered to be a foe was really your friend.

An exchange will take place pending your arrival. You will lay down a cross and put on a crown, only to cast it at His feet. Coronation is no longer important, as you behold the Lamb of God. Peel off the armor and pull out the thorn, the pilgrimage is over. Welcome home.

Chapter Four

EARTH ANGELS

Most men will proclaim every one his own good-ness: but a faithful man who can find? (Proverbs 20:6)

The church service had turned out okay. The pastor inquired if I was hungry and offered to take me for a bite to eat. I wasn't, so I politely declined his invitation and returned to my room, exhausted from preaching back-to-back crusades. I purposely double-book weekends sometimes, which allows me to take a couple weeks off and spend time with my family. I begin a meeting on Friday evening and go through Sunday morning, then move to another congregation Sunday evening and stay until Tuesday evening. Then there are occasions when I minister solely on Sundays, because my body can't keep up with this demanding schedule.

I am usually an early riser, but this particular evening I decided not to request a wake-up call; nor did I bother to activate my inner alarm. You and I both are wondering if we really do have such a thing. But whenever I have to catch an early flight, almost without fail, I wake up before the buzzer goes off.

I made a quick call home to touch base and make sure all was well. My daughters both said they had a so-so day at school. I prayed with them and told them how I looked forward to seeing them in a couple days.

I have stayed at probably every hotel chain in America, everything from Motel 6 to Marriott and Ramada to Ritz Carlton, but I have yet to encounter one that compares with the comfort of home. I am happiest when I sip coffee out of *my* mug, lounge in *my* recliner, lay *my* head on *my* pillow, and sleep in *my* bed. Of course being in the company of my family tops the list. Also, my wife is a meticulous housekeeper and knows how to prepare a scrumptious meal.

With the room cool and pitch dark, I turned off my cell phone and drifted off to sleep. Anyone who tried to contact me would have to wait. I just wanted to stay beneath the covers without any disturbance. With people and duties pulling at me all the time, this is not easy to do. So, when I have the opportunity, I take advantage of it.

Nothing unusual happened: no premonitions, no nightmares. It was actually a very peaceful night, and as I recall, I drifted off to sleep rather quickly. Morning came and I fumbled for the remote and tuned into ABC, and that's when everything changed. I couldn't believe my eyes. My first thought was that this was a replay of a past event. Uh! Uh! This was not Oklahoma City and this was not the Federal Murah building. As terrible and tragic as that horrific disaster was, it paled in comparison to what was now happening.

I detected a quiver in Peter Jennings' voice and distinctly recall hearing him say that what was happening was *unbelievable*. Anchormen are trained to avoid using such words and from showing emotion in times of crisis so as not to proliferate the anxiety of the viewers. However, in this situation protocol was not important—everyone was bewildered. The world wept and wondered.

We would later learn that militant Muslim extremists, using domestic airlines laden with passengers and fuel, had attacked the twin 110-story towers

The masterminds of cruelty had discovered our vulnerability. They calmly boarded our passenger planes, overpowered the flight crews, and turned them into enormous missiles with wings.

of the World Trade Center in New York City. The shining city on the hill had been penetrated by evil, and our immunity from anarchy had failed. Oceans no longer provided resistance from aggression. The masterminds of cruelty had discovered our vulnerability. They calmly boarded our passenger planes, overpowered the flight crews, and turned them into enormous missiles with wings.

Suddenly breaking news came from Washington, DC, stating that the Pentagon had just been hit. Almost simultaneously an announcement was made that an airliner had gone down in a field in rural Pennsylvania. Now, the news anchorman was saying something about two F-16s being scrambled to intercept an aircraft headed for the White House or the U.S. Capitol Building.

All the major networks were broadcasting the same events. As I lay catching up on much needed rest, history was being made. My mind seemed to go numb and I became fixated on the news. I switched on my cell phone and saw several messages had been placed on my voice-mail, all from my wife. I dialed home and spoke with her. She informed me that one of our daughters had called home from school crying, worrying if Dad would make it home safely.

I instructed her to go immediately to the bank in order to have cash on hand, go to the supermarket and stock up on water and nonperishable food, and fill the Jeep up with gas. I was neither paranoid nor apocalyptic but felt it was prudent to be prepared for worst-case scenario, whatever that would entail. In the event there was a run on banks and grocery stores, I wanted to make sure my family had ample provisions. Amid the pandemonium, my wife, Marilyn, maintained remarkable composure.

Then it was time for me to plan an alternate means of returning to Texas. I knew that I would not be returning on Delta Airlines as I had arrived. I wanted to get home as quickly as possible to comfort my children and calm their fears. My dilemma was solved when a couple attending the crusade offered to drive me the five hours from North Little Rock to Plano.

With my transportation for getting back home taken care of, I laid down the phone and returned to the news. I stared at the television with mouth agape. What a contrast: Black billowing clouds of smoke ascending from lower Manhattan, and in the foreground, lovely Lady Liberty, extending that imposing radiant torch. I know statues have no consciousness, but she seemed to epitomize the steadfast resolve of America. She still embraces the tired, poor, and huddled masses yearning to breathe free. Hate does not possess the capability to smother the inextinguishable flame of freedom.

September 11, 2001 was the day the world experienced a paradigm shift. Heroes were not just those who gained yardage, made touchdowns, scored goals, or starred on the silver screen. Those brave men and women of the FDNY, NYPD, and EMS emerged from the extreme edges of obscurity and took center stage in our hearts.

The infidels failed miserably in their mission. Rather than divide, these barbaric acts made America that much more cohesive. We finally laid down our prejudices; ethnicity and skin color were no longer important. Democrat and Republican senators stood abreast on the steps of the U.S. Capitol Building, singing "God Bless America." I wept openly as network news showed footage of the U.S. national anthem being played at Buckingham Palace in London and the Canadian Parliament in Ottawa.

The resiliency of this great nation radiated through dense clouds of catastrophe as money poured into charitable organizations, surpassing one billion dollars. The Red Cross was inundated with long lines of people, who sometimes waited for six hours to donate blood. Some were actually told to return in a couple of weeks due to the staggering response.

The unprecedented expressions of patriotism from coast to coast were overwhelming. One didn't venture far from home before spotting an American flag. I, like millions of others in America, didn't have to leave my residence to catch a glimpse of the star spangled banner. The first thing I noticed when I finally returned home was the red, white, and blue, (colors that don't run) softly streaming in the warm Texas breeze. After my darling wife made her rounds she slipped into Kmart and purchased one of the rapidly vanishing flags. I remain a proud Canadian who is extremely grateful to be living in the good ole USA.

Wednesday evening, September 12, the atmosphere at the Bustard house was solemn as we recounted the previous eventful 24 hours. There was no logical explanation as to how people could commit such atrocities on their fellow human beings. It all served as a reminder of the evil present in our world.

I tried not to think of my upcoming schedule. I didn't want to leave, but not because of fear; I just wanted to be with my family. One part of me wanted to take up arms and stand abreast of the young men and women of our military and defend the honor of America.

The Faithful Brave

A generation plagued with scandals, scams, and scoundrels realized that true heroes still exist. They didn't just suddenly appear on this fateful September day; they were always there, in the panorama, risking their lives every day. I confess my negligence in acknowledging just how vital and perilous their occupations are. I since have gained a profound appreciation, and will be eternally grateful for their daily sacrifice.

This rare breed of humanity is not adored because of multimillion-dollar contracts awarded for athletic ability, but because they demonstrate uncommon valor. They go far beyond the call of duty. On September 11 many of them paid the ultimate price. As Jesus said, "Greater love hath no man than this, that a man lay down his life for his friends" (Jn. 15:13).

These courageous policemen and firemen who ran into the collapsing World Trade Center Towers were not psychologically unstable. They were mentally competent and physically fit, and performed precisely as they were trained. They shoved feelings and family into the background of their minds, and focused their energy and attention on the disaster at hand. Were they afraid? Terrified! Did they want to enter these deadly infernos? Of course not! Then why'd they do it? Drive to your local fire station and ask. I am not about to display indignity in attempting to answer the inquiry. I wasn't cut from the impervious piece of fabric they were and I am unqualified to comment on the subject.

Time magazine ran a photo of a fireman ascending the stairwell in one of the towers. A woman who was rushing to escape had come face-to-face with him on one of the landings. The mere thought of the picture causes it to surface vividly in my mind.

> These courageous policemen and firemen who ran into the collapsing World Trade Center Towers were not psychologically unstable. They were mentally competent and physically fit, and performed precisely as they were trained.

His helmet appeared to be hanging on the side of his head, held by the strap under his chin. His coat seemed to be slipping off his right shoulder. Soot covered his face and his eyes were opened wide with excitement. I caught a glimpse of the uncertainty that must have gripped him.

It seemed to me that his countenance read: *I know I won't be going home after my shift. There'll be no supper with the family, no watching the evening news in my easy chair, no tucking the kids in and sharing a quiet moment with my wife.* He bounded up those stairs with all his strength, hoping to rescue someone who would get to do what he might not be able to ever again.

On November 3 another disaster occurred. Only this time there were no terrorists and, for that matter, no enemies. Two departments who had worked in concert were now squared off against each other. Mayor Giuliani had given his approval to cut the number of rescuers searching the rubble for remains, and for the use of heavy equipment to remove mass quantities of wreckage.

The firefighters became livid. This gargantuan heap of cement and steel was hallowed ground to them. The bodies of their comrades lay among the debris. "Bring the brothers out, bring the brothers out!" shouted the angry firefighters as they marched together toward the barricades. To them it would be, as one of them put it, "blasphemy" to remove the debris any other way than by hand, carefully examining each crevice for body parts.

In the scuffle twelve firemen were arrested and five policemen injured. I felt sick to my stomach as I watched this unfortunate situation transpire. I stood in the Cincinnati airport and shook my head over the news. These were outstanding, passionate men with inflamed emotions. Their allegiance never diminished as they shouted, in that distinct New York accent, "They're our brothers."

America is admonished to stay vigilant in case of another terrorist strike. Homeland Security Chief Tom Ridge says another attack is inevitable. There's no question that our country has been unnerved after these dastardly deeds. Life will never be the same as we guard our borders and skies, and inoculate against bio-terrorism. But I believe the country sleeps better after witnessing the bravery demonstrated at the World Trade Center and the Pentagon. I'll work diligently to never take this exceptional class of people for granted again, and am reminded of them every time I hear the blare of a siren.

The world would be much more hazardous without heroes. Wars have been won, tyranny vanquished, and freedom gained because of men and women who lay down their lives. We all watched in horror that day as those two lofty symbols of prosperity collapsed, but then we observed the giants who ascended from the ruins.

Inconspicuous Giants

Some heroes are never discovered for centuries and then perhaps inadvertently, their valiancy is unearthed and tribute is conferred. Something is added to all of us each time a missing page of history is replaced in the encyclopedia of heroics, and we become better because of it.

Acts of bravery are not just constituted by taking up arms, or entering burning buildings. Throughout dispensations and generations, there have always been selfless, cross-bearing, second-mile men and women who contributed to a cause, took a stand, and bore the heat. There is such a case in Scripture. If it were not for this inconspicuous, humble gentleman, you and

I would not enjoy this new life we have come to cherish. A brief portrait of this nebulous individual is depicted in the Gospels. He was actually a primary participant, but because his character was eclipsed by others who were more prominent one really doesn't get a complete description of him. It's sort of like the kid's contest—*Where's Waldo?*

The vast economy of God's Kingdom is positively re-markable in its variety of subjects. It is a comprehensive prism through which one views another example of the diversity of God. We all hale from different backgrounds; we all bring bag-gage, regardless of how impressive our portfolios might be. God rejects no one, but instead, places each into a slot that has every indication it was uniquely tailored for that one individual.

Our heavenly Father is the most ingenious engineer. He can mine worthless ore from mountainous heaps of iniquity, smelt and refine it, and then develop it into something mag-nificent. What others consider slag, He deems useful. All of humanity is included in the thought process of God.

It is sort of an eternal drama, a celestial cinema if you please, where one enters the stage in a predetermined scene. Whether the role insinuates importance or insignificance, we simply do our best in the theater of life. The script embraces romance, redemption, passion, and mystery, and the final scene is simply out of this world. Whether intelligent or inept, no one is ignored on the casting couch and passed over for someone more promising. All are invited to participate in the greatest love story ever written.

Some 2,000 years ago a member of the cast emerged from behind the curtain and made a brief appearance. The role undoubtedly required a special person. A rare kind of meekness was necessary for the one who would play this part.

The great Playwright carefully made the selection from a vast array of candidates. Where would God look to find such a person to fit the part? More than likely, not many would want it. But a humble carpenter from a tiny Galilean town was chosen. His role: to be the stepdad of Christ.

All of my ministerial life, spanning some 20 years, I have preached that God does not impose upon the will of man. I have relayed, in somewhat of an amusing way, how God did not make Jonah go to Ninevah, but rather made him want to go to Ninevah. Jonah could have stepped from the ship onto the pier, but instead was belched onto the beach by a whale (see Jon. 2:10). After all, we are free moral agents. It really is up to the individual to agree or disagree.

However, I find nowhere in Scripture where God consulted with Joseph, Mary's fiancé, and explained the finer points of his and her involvement in the grand scheme of things, the details of which were unquestionably significant.

Have you ever imagined how such a meeting might have happened? God declares to Joseph, "I am going to use the womb of your future wife as an incubator to birth the only begotten Son of God. Of course, this will cause the both of you almost unbearable strife. Mary's sanitary reputation will be stained. She will have to endure gossip, evade zealots, and pay an enormous price.

"And you, Joseph, will have to exercise courageous faith. On some occasions the Boy's life will depend upon your ability to be in tune with the Spirit. When the time comes for you to know Mary intimately you will have to abstain for several months so that what the prophets spoke can be fulfilled: Jesus would be born of a virgin (see Is. 7:14). This unprecedented move of God will invade your home, your workshop, and every facet of your life."

Joseph didn't ask for this! He didn't submit an application to be the guardian of God. There he was, in his modest woodshop minding his business, just doing his thing, when boom: "Joseph, this is Jehovah! You're not too busy for the next 33 years, are you? Mary is the one I am really interested in. That doesn't mean I will not be requiring your services. Someone has to help Mary look after and raise the Boy."

Mary received a noteworthy accolade. However, the same is not stated of Joseph. I understand his limited involvement; still I would argue he couldn't be dismissed as merely a prop.

And the angel came in unto her, and said, Hail, thou that art highly favored, the Lord is with thee: blessed art thou among women (Luke 1:28).

Imagine having your life commandeered in such a way; talk about cramping your style. The finite is no match for the Infinite, so there is no sense in entering debate. Perhaps the only choice you have is to go along or move along. History's unrivaled event is dawning and you have been swept into the vortex.

Just who is this man whom God deemed worthy to be the custodian of Christ? He surely must have possessed extraordinary characteristics to meet the prerequisites. I know of two young ladies who consider me to be an overprotective dad!

What my beautiful daughters need to realize is that I value them as priceless treasures. Their well-being is my priority. I have found myself more than once wondering how these darlings came into my life!

Being a dad from a distance is not an easy task, but thanks to a cell phone and e-mail, I communicate with my family several times each day. Being dad is a given, but maintaining status as a close friend is something I work at continually.

My wife and I have always been very discriminating as to who baby-sat our children when we had to be away. Considering that one in four children suffer abuse, one cannot be too careful. We keep abreast of their friends and acquaintances to ensure good company and a healthy environment. When they venture from the nest, their mother and I can only hope that we have instilled good morals that will guide them through life's capricious journey.

The Gospels do not offer much information about Joseph. Some historians have suggested that he was somewhat older than Mary and that accounts for his meekness. My opinion is, regardless of Joseph's age he most likely would be meek. It is an element of his inherent nature.

When one considers the list of the champions of faith, Joseph should definitely be listed somewhere close to the top of the page. He opts to stay with Mary, although she is with child, because he is told in a dream that this is a God thing (see Mt. 1:20). It doesn't matter what the advice of his close friends may be; he will remain with the young lady.

Why doesn't he push for his rights to be acknowledged? In today's sue-crazy society, where everyone wants justice, he would have a legitimate beef! Just maybe he has a right to stand Mary in the door of her father's house and have her stoned (see Deut. 22:21)! After all, that was quite an explanation she gave as to how this all came to pass. *The Holy what caused this?*

Surrendering to Sovereignty

I am aware that in this post-baby-boom generation what I'm writing may be offensive but I am going to indulge myself anyhow. If you are more concerned about yourself and exercising all of your rights, *bless God*! You haven't bowed to the sovereignty of the Spirit.

I have polled audiences attending the crusades I ministered in with this question: "When was the last time you heard a life-changing sermon on the sovereignty of God?" No one has supplied a reference, and my answer is mutual. Is there such a thing anymore as "Not my will, but Thine be done"? Just because Heaven paid a premium price for me, does God have a right to expect my best?

If being an itinerant evangelist becomes boring, can I change my modus operandi? Do I really have to *sell out* to the cause of God? Do I have the luxury of retaining collateral and thus not be expected to be entirely His?

Had Joseph aspirations of being a superstar, he would not have accepted this role. Superstars feel worthy of leading roles, and certainly are not into making cameo appearances. A part like this does not allow one to be nominated for an Academy Award. No getting measured for outrageously-priced tailored garments. No stepping to the podium and clutching an Oscar for a minor part such as this.

I pose a question to you, the reader: In this modern era of Christianity, which enjoys mammoth sanctuaries and cutting-edge ministries, attended by thousands of faithful parishioners, is there a need for those who will work behind the scenes, experiencing little if no recognition? Are there people who do not demand attention and accolades, but are content to fill whatever position may be vacant? Should the Lord call such people to operate within the parameters of the fivefold ministry, they are willing, but would be much more comfortable in a less visible role?

Are there those who afford God such preeminence that He can invade any part of their lives whenever He so chooses? Whether it is their marriage, home, or business, He can step in and perform His will. These divine interruptions sometimes drastically alter the landscape until it is completely opposite of what we may have dreamed of.

What about the hopes and aspirations of Joseph? I am sure he had plans of where he would live and how many children he would have; a future that included his and Mary's retiring from his carpentry shop at a comfortable age. He probably had a spot picked out where he and Mary would enjoy their twilight years. Joseph was probably someone who took calculated steps, always looking ahead. As the head of the household I would only think it proper that he emphasized a few things he desired.

What magnificent meekness! I understand this is an oxymoron but it seems so appropriate in describing the personality of Joseph. This man even forfeited his right to name the lad. He made no demands that He be named Joe Junior; if His name was to be Jesus, thus it was! Joseph's primary purpose may very well have been that he was the first human to speak that hallowed, matchless name—*Jesus* (see Mt. 1:25).

What a rare specimen of the male population Joseph must have been! Here was a guy who was so surrendered to the sovereignty of the Holy Spirit that he stepped aside and allowed Heaven to invade every avenue of his life. He didn't try to negotiate a better deal for himself. If he didn't get to take center stage, that was all right with him. Not many dads are willing to play second fiddle in their own homes.

Unity's Enchanting Symphony

In order for an opus to be performed correctly by the symphony, every musician must be in perfect harmony. The percussion, strings, and horns, precisely tuned, must watch attentively and follow the baton of the conductor. Obviously not all will get to play the solo or the bridge, but every instrument is needed. The twelfth-chair violinist must practice for endless hours and attend every rehearsal just like the first-chair violinist.

These talented people who run through repetitive drills for hours on end until they finally get it right, do so because of a fervent passion to make beautiful music with the rest of the team. The most technologically advanced stereo cannot communicate the spirit of the symphony. When one attends a live performance he or she observes what ears alone cannot capture: the countenance of the musicians as they feel every lyric they play.

Many instruments issue sounds that cannot be distinguished apart from the entirety of the orchestra, but the reason your spirit is enraptured by the music is attributed to the fact that everyone on the stage is playing his or her part.

If an orchestra was composed of only those who play first-chair, there would be no depth; every piece played would sound monotone. But the diversity of instruments and musicians affords a superb sound. Behind the Mozarts, Mahlers, and Chopins are accomplished musicians who have devoted their lives to making music. They stay attentive to do their part, whether it is a stroke on the strings, a blast from a trumpet, or a single clash of the cymbals. Without such people, a composition would remain lifeless on paper. Their names are not placed on the marquis, but instead remain unspoken. However, the most capable conductor cannot summon one sound without their presence.

Ludwig Von Beethoven is a celebrated name among composers. However, if his concertos are to be played, many unnamed musicians must participate. Of course Beethoven intentionally included them when he drafted the compositions. So it is with God. It's not that we are indispensable; He could have sung His song all by Himself. Instead He deliberately wrote a heavenly hymn that called for a choir and not a soloist.

I guess you're wondering what the title of this *heavenly hymn* is—"Saved by Grace"! It's the song of the Lamb (see Rev. 15:3), written throughout dispensations and centuries, and throughout the ages of patriarchs, judges, prophets, and kings.

I am fascinated with Bible characters who performed impressive feats and yet whose names remain a mystery—history's unsung heroes! Although their exploits merited notation, they themselves remain cloaked in anonymity.

The name Jonathan (son of Saul) appears over one hundred times in Scripture. He's a blueblood! The son of a king! But the reason he was victorious at the garrison of the Philistines is because a young man we simply know as his *armor-bearer* endangered his own life in order to sustain a victory (see 1 Sam. 14:1-13).

The Bible provides geographical names, which allow us to comprehend Jonathan's strategy: the element of surprise. He chose an almost impassible route due to the rugged terrain (see 1 Sam. 14:4-5). This minor detail makes the story much more intriguing. Does the region justify identifying him and not the dauntless armor-bearer?

This dangerous venture that will make Jonathan look good in the eyes of his countrymen may cost the armor-bearer his own life. The armor-bearer does not inquire if his name will merit recognition for assisting in the battle. There is no animosity on his part toward Jonathan and his status. An armor-bearer's life is not as valuable as that of the son of a king, and the lad knows it. If the armor-bearer dies in combat, Israel will not mourn over the loss of him as they would over the death of Jonathan.

When the dust settles, if they survive this skirmish, they'll go back to their individual lives. Jonathan will return to the castle and the armor-bearer to his quarters. He doesn't get to hang out, just help out. He won't be mingling with the upper echelons of society. He knows his place, and has no problem with it. He and Jonathan will reunite when another conflict arises. He remains just as dedicated to Israel's cause as Jonathan.

This is a man who Jonathan has deemed worthy of his confidence. He has commissioned him with the task of accompanying him onto the battlefield. He is selected because of his skill and gallantry. He is the last wall of defense between the son of a king and malevolent adversaries. His loyalty is unquestionable and his resolve inflexible. The armor-bearer has united his heart with Jonathan's.

> *And his armourbearer said unto him, Do all that is in thine heart: turn thee; behold, I am with thee according to thy heart* (1 Samuel 14:7).

The Din of Silence

I implore someone to explain to me *when* Joseph exited stage right. I have read a few assumptions. The answer remains unknown. He must have departed before Calvary. If Joseph was alive on that horrific day there is no way that Jesus would have asked the beloved disciple to take Mary to his own house (see Jn. 19:27). It would have been Joseph's bosom Mary rested her face upon. Joseph's consolation and compassion would have sustained Mary after the tragic death of her eldest son, helping her to survive the heartbreaking experience.

He didn't cop out along the way. A man who possesses trustworthy character of this caliber doesn't suddenly mutate into a delinquent. He executed his role masterfully and then softly strolled off stage into the evening shadows. Apparently there were no standing ovations, no curtain calls. Like fog dissipating in the morning sunlight, he vanished into oblivion.

People like Joseph speak loudly without opening their mouths, but are not obnoxious. They never interrupt and are only heard when yielded to. They have a subtle way of portraying minor roles and acquiring attention. Something about their mild personalities captivates the beholder.

To what do I attribute this? The Josephs remind us of ourselves. That's us off in the distant background, making a minimal contribution in a supporting role. When we're in the company of certain people we feel as if we're Piper Cubs, taxiing alongside Concordes. Perhaps the invitations were mailed to the wrong address and we're actually here by mistake.

Our names are not household words. We're not anticipating receiving any awards. We're humbled at the thought of being considered to participate in any capacity. We don't require trumpets announcing our arrival or our departure. There's no one on the payroll managing our fan clubs.

We don't become irate, questioning why we were given a lesser status than others. There's no need to study the script; one doesn't have to strain to learn to recite *one* sentence. We are well aware that anyone could take our place and do a better job. We don't retreat to our dressing rooms where our names are placed directly under our stars.

We don't necessitate traveling with a security detail. We'll never be thronged by admirers nor pursued by paparazzi. We won't boycott if the salary is inadequate. Actually, we feel undeserving of any compensation. We're elated that we've been invited.

> *For a day in Thy courts is better than a thousand. I had rather be a doorkeeper in the house of my God, than to dwell in the tents of wickedness* (Psalm 84:10).

I'm reminded of an aphorism spoken by Saint Francis of Assisi: "Preach the gospel. When necessary, use words." These are the homilies that warrant the greatest response: people who don't utter a word, but speak volumes with their sincerity.

Joseph's character is eclipsed by Christ throughout the Scriptures. Obscurity seems to be his lot in life. The name of his wife is still mentioned by millions on a daily basis. His meekness does not suggest a lack of masculinity. I don't believe he had a spine made out of angel-hair pasta. Instead, I believe he was the backbone of the family.

Is there the slightest possibility that some of the meekness found in Jesus was actually imparted by Joseph? Was his obedience to the Spirit a role model for humanity's obedience to deity? I am glad that along with the list of valiant soldiers and vanguards of the faith mentioned in Scripture, there is a gentle giant named Joseph. He recognized a divine move of God in his life and never offered any resistance.

We know that Joseph was not chosen simply by coincidence. A case can be made for the requisite being his exemplary life. James, the half-brother of Jesus and son of Joseph, adds credence to this line of thinking. Not only is James a noticeable figure in the New Testament Church, it is obvious the apostle Paul held James in high regard.

I am glad that along with the list of valiant soldiers and vanguards of the faith mentioned in Scripture, there is a gentle giant named Joseph. He recognized a divine move of God in his life and never offered any resistance.

"Children project human qualities upon God. The characteristics of God are closely related to experiences children have had with their parents. Children's experiences with their fathers lay the groundwork for future conceptions about what God is like."[3]

Let's Hear It for the Stagehands!

I know of a few who come close to attaining this kind of spiritual stature today. Being overwhelmed with compassion for those who have not heard the wondrous gospel, they surrender to the bidding of the Spirit and embark on their mission. Whether it is in a distant land populated by heathens, or walking among rows of cells in a maximum-security penitentiary, they obediently spread the story of Jesus.

These facets of ministry are not rewarded with luxury autos and Caribbean condos. Nor do they receive invitations to minister at international conferences. I salute my colleagues who faithfully carry the gospel to the incarcerated, and to missionaries who forsake the creature comforts of home, leaving behind friends and family, to spread the hope of eternal life.

I also want to pay homage to the devout who minister through their works, not their words. They are the Marthas who ensure sustenance and stability. They labor long hours behind the curtain, receiving little if no recognition, unlike those on stage, who curtsy to lauding fans after a brief performance. They're never petitioned for autographs but endorse their efforts with excellence.

There are occasions when menial chores translate into momentous assignments. Take Philip for example. He went from waiting on tables to preaching a citywide revival in Samaria. Of course in those days, high standards were set for waiters (see Acts 6:1-3): They had to be of honest report, full of the Holy Ghost, and full of wisdom.

I've been eating all my life but have never stumbled into a diner this divine. I wonder if the food would require being blessed. Sorry, couldn't resist! It does, however, give us an idea of the emphasis the early Church placed on service.

But when thou doest alms, let not thy left hand know what thy right hand doeth: that thine alms may be in secret: and thy Father which seeth in secret Himself shall reward thee openly (Matthew 6:3-4).

As I reflect on my years of service in the ministry, I have not a single regret. I am not hinting that my road has been extremely rough. There have been a few bumps along the way, but I don't regret one mile of this journey. God is a wonderful boss! The benefits are fantastic and the retirement is out of this world.

Hopefully, this chapter has afforded you a perspective of Joseph that has been enlightening. Was there any acknowledgment made of his modest contribution? You bet! Stay in your seat and read the list of cast members. As you peruse the credits you will stumble onto the name of Joseph, stepdad of Christ. Yeah, it's there. Etched into the lineage of Jesus is the name of the devoted, dutiful, and docile man whose participation helped make salvation possible. That's what I call making your notch in the tree (see Lk. 3:23).

I feel certain that on the day when rewards are distributed, I will step aside to allow the saints who may have revered me, access to the One who sits upon the throne. They did not preach their sermons over a pulpit, but lived them throughout their lives. The spotlight never captured their profile, because they worked behind the scenes.

They were there all along. It's kind of like a 3-D picture: You have to look past the first impressions of myriad colors, lines, and patterns. As you peer through the picture, another emerges. Within the abstract scenes of life that make very little sense, are hidden the few, the proud, the brave. There is an exhilarating sensation as they appear larger than life.

Wow! As you concentrate on keeping the inner image focused, you are amazed at its reality. More details are revealed as you continue to allow your vision to drift. Same way with heroes! Before skyscrapers became collapsing infernos, trapping thousands, they were there. The horror did not create the hero. Within the unimaginable devastation were men and women performing valiantly.

Below is a brief list of the many overlooked modern-day heroes. They are the underpaid professionals who evaluate their vocation as much more than just a job. They are unnoticed on life's flamboyant surface, but if you readjust your vision, you'll catch a glimpse of people who make life much better.

- Educators: Every professional athlete, celebrity, musician, singer, etc. had a teacher who instilled ethics as well as education. Unfortunately the marketplace has dictated teachers' salaries to be much less than many of their former students.

- Caregivers: On swollen feet, with aching backs, caregivers attend to the incoherent and incapacitated, as if they were their own. They take the time to lend an ear to the lonely and forgotten, while lifting bodies and emptying bedpans.

- Sunday school teachers: As if their schedules weren't crammed already, they prepare all week to impact young lives with biblical truths. Demonstrating God's unconditional love, they embrace each child, whether rascal or role model.

- Volunteers: Whether attending city council meetings or serving soup kitchens, they strive to keep crime low and neighborly kindness high. Some volunteers even become big brothers to mentor boys who are minus a dad.

- Doctors: Some take well-deserved vacations to third-world countries. Instead of lounging around luxurious resorts, they care for the impoverished free of charge. They bring hope to hostile lands, putting smiles on faces once covered with flies.

- Passengers on United Airlines, Flight 93: Many phoned home bidding farewell. They cited the Lord's prayer, then announced, "Let's roll." They thwarted perpetrators of evil from committing further carnage in our country.

> May these precious patriots rest in peace. We
> remain forever indebted to their sacrifice.

I have to conclude with the roster before the chapter becomes the book. My mind is brimming with numerous examples of everyday people doing extraordinary things. The fact is, devout people who perform noteworthy deeds surround us. They are immersed in their duties and consider recognition inappropriate. To them it's nothing more than doing their job. Readjust your vision and they will come into view like Easter lilies amid autumn foliage, which begs the question: How did I overlook them?

We need to keep an eye out for heroes. If we make this our practice it won't necessitate a catastrophe to discover the devoted. Heroes are never ostentatious and don't wear eccentric costumes, soaring high in the sky. They're earth angels, glistening amid gloominess, appearing ordinary, but possessing incomparable audacity. Although they have cherubic attributes, they maintain a unique way of touching their fellowman.

Stay alert, because everyday heroes don't employ spokespeople to tip off the media and broadcast their presence. Magazine correspondents trying to get the jump on a scoop don't invade their privacy. One more thing: They're easily embarrassed when attention is bestowed. They're not infatuated over stardom, so don't elevate them to pedestals. Their commitment to you exceeds your admiration of them.

Chapter Five

NECESSARY EVIL

*Fight the good fight of faith, lay hold on eternal life,
whereunto thou art also called, and hast professed
a good profession before many witnesses* (1 Timothy
6:12).

You have finally finished your tenure in the wastelands,
walked through dry riverbeds, and implanted your footprints
into the terra firma of your promised land. The day you
thought would never arrive has dawned. The joy in just standing here is overwhelming. Many times you wept from midnight to daylight, then got up and encouraged yourself to keep
pushing onward. Teetering on the threshold of exhaustion you
convinced your wobbly legs to carry you on.

The continual grumbling from your companions was like an
excruciating toothache. It gnawed on your nerves steadily. Toler-
ating those crude circumstances was difficult enough. Adding
chronic complainers to the mix made it almost insufferable.

Opportunities to turn back invariably presented themselves to you. The loneliness became an almost unbearable
yoke at times. The living conditions on occasion would try
even the most adept explorer, and Lewis or Clark you're not.

Awakening at daybreak to collect your daily rations grew increasingly tedious. A little variety in the menu would have been a welcome treat. Manna du jour/365 for 40 years? You tried to be creative but how many different dishes can one prepare using such bland ingredients?

The fear of the unknown weighed heavily upon you as you slowly migrated toward a place you had only heard of. More nights than you can recall were spent struggling to grasp a few moments of sleep. Just like the weightless gray fluff of a fading dandelion borne on a mild breeze, rest proved too evasive.

You always felt like a transient as the uncertainty of a desolate existence took its toll. Frankly, you never did fit in. You were a stranger roving through a foreign land. An intrinsic tenacity compelled you to succeed and would not permit you to put down roots in the desert. You refused to let yourself become attached to inferior surroundings. This is noteworthy considering many people akin to you failed to transcend their environment.

Half of your life is already behind you and has seeped into the Saharan sands of yore. You realize everything you've heard about midlife crisis is accurate as you reexamine the few accomplishments to your credit. At this stage of the game one should have his or her game plan in order, but here you are pioneering a brand new life.

Thinking about all the changes incites a nagging insecurity. You always were a systematic sort. Over the decades you laid out comprehensive blueprints, but now you catch yourself deep in thought, deliberating as to how long it will take to become acclimated to the milieu.

You came face-to-face with insurmountable odds. The only thing that provided consolation was the legend, passed down from previous generations of a miraculous emancipation. At times you wondered if it was just a far-fetched fable. There must be some veracity to it: You made it through.

God severed impenetrable obstacles; breathed upon the deep waters of constraint, creating a transparent corridor; gently took you by the hand; and led you through. Only you and God are aware of the magnitude of your redemption.

Your mind is tired from wrestling—wrestling with questions like: Is all this necessary and will it be worth it? You stand overlooking expansive loamy acreage and a sense of being home envelops you. It seems ridiculous that people could feel indigenous to a country they have never seen.

As you survey the rolling pastures of your utopia you realize it's everything you dreamed it would be and a whole lot more. Every direction you look, you notice bountiful blessings that God assured were yours. Wow! Just look at those flourishing vineyards and splendid gardens. One day of splendor causes 40 years of hardship to vanish. You're thankful you didn't terminate the journey during those strenuous years.

Mixed emotions spring from a soul that has only known affliction. Tears trickle down your dusty cheek, sliding along the contours of the broad grin on your face. You need to write a note and mail it to the members of the flat-earth society who tried to discourage your voyage.

The hike through the desert was difficult. Your friends thought you were deranged. You were always talking about crossing over and stepping into a land of plenty, continually fanning the flame that emblazoned your spirit with passion. *Poor soul, behind every silver lining there's a cloud. Maybe one day he'll come down to earth. One day he'll wake up from those impractical fantasies.* Who's laughing now?

Rejoicing is not out of order. You have earned the right to express your gratefulness in the most demonstrative manner you choose. Besides, this is a land of jubilation. You have left the mournful past, which at its best was a subsistence, enslaving you to brutal taskmasters.

Trouble in Paradise

Oh, so you're not rejoicing; you're baffled! You've discovered walls of hindrance and giants of opposition. Now that you are on location, you realize there are some major matters that merit your attention. All your life you kept marching by faith and stomping on doubt. Now that you have entered what you considered to be your destiny, you need clarification as to why enemies are living on the premises of your promise. Problems in paradise? Go figure!

- After much supplication and waiting on God you embarked on establishing a church in the city He directed you to. The benediction for the inaugural service hadn't been offered when hell placed a leaflet on your doorstep stating plans to oust your fledgling flock.

- You launched a new business venture, promising God that your business was actually His business. Your ambition was to become a financier of the Kingdom. But guess who was first in line for your grand opening? The devil must have seen the flyer and set about to shut you down.

- You isolated yourself for a season of spiritual renewal. Denying your flesh inspired your spirit. Just when the inward was conquered you were confronted by evil on the outward. I think I read of this before!

It would be refreshing to have a little reprieve from trouble. You haven't just spent "hell week" training with the Navy Seals. You haven't been engaging in covert exercises with the Special Ops. You have been eking out a life on the grueling sands of a barren wilderness. You certainly don't distinguish yourself as a powerful warrior who is armed and dangerous.

It was an uphill struggle to get here. When does a person get to relish in leisure? Why is it that we are shoved into another conflict just as the current one is ending? Before your entourage hoists you to their shoulders another challenger steps into the ring.

Since everything God does is with a divine purpose, you and I should examine this closely and determine why God didn't exterminate these adversaries before your arrival. We know He is not a demented dictator who gets thrills out of watching His children battle the diabolical regiments of darkness.

If you think testing was only for yesterday you are mistaken. God sees you now as the futuristic figure He wants you to become.

Please understand this is a land of champions, not a kindergarten for immature Christians. If you think testing was only for yesterday, you are mistaken. God sees you now as the futuristic figure He wants you to become. He understands that resistance is necessary for your spiritual progression. He loves you so much that He refuses to leave you in your undeveloped stage. He blessed you with an adversary to help you achieve your full potential.

Blessed with an adversary? Now that is a contradictory statement! Actually, it isn't. The fact is, despite a prestigious surname and an array of assets that one may inherit, hard times inevitably knock on every door, regardless if one dwells in a lofty penthouse or a dilapidated trailer-house. It is up to each individual to determine if it becomes his or her elimination or edification.

If thou faint in the day of adversity, thy strength is small (Proverbs 24:10).

Necessary Evil

In a perfect world there would be no devil. Imagine living without iniquity, disease and distress, and never having to subdue your carnality while fighting off lewd temptations. It would be wonderful not to have to continually expel evil thoughts from your mind.

It would be marvelous to hear about benevolence instead of violence and serenity instead of hostility. If only every nation in the Middle East could embrace a permanent treaty rather than irrepressible malice. Earth will continue to be like an unstable bottle of nitroglycerine until Christ returns.

Being in the Church doesn't provide immunity from the misdeeds of evildoers in this present world. You may be new in the Kingdom but already you understand this isn't Eden. Someone once alluded to Christians always needing an enemy. It isn't by our choosing. It doesn't take very long for a new convert to perceive this is not for the faint of heart.

> Someone once alluded to Christians always needing an enemy. It isn't by our choosing. It doesn't take very long for a new convert to perceive this is not for the faint of heart.

A dear minister friend asked God the $64,000 question: "God, why did You allow lucifer to become a devil?" The Lord answered him saying, "I did it for you. Think of all the answers to prayers you've received, the victories you've won, and the miracles you have witnessed."

You and I both agree that the original intent of God was not to have a ruthless renegade terrorizing His greatest creation. But, since lucifer rebelled, the permissive will of God was enacted. God chose not to annihilate satan, but instead allowed him limited access to His children.

When the conflict is furious and it appears you're losing, it is imperative to remember that satan is on a leash. He cannot run roughshod over your home and pilfer everything in your possession whenever he desires. God has established regulations, and satan along with the rest of creation must abide by them.

The purpose of God allowing an antagonist entry into specific areas of our lives is not to leave us maimed and endure the remainder of our days disabled. Rather, it is to produce strength that is attained only through testing.

Physical muscles are developed through resistance; the same can be said concerning the anatomy of the spirit. When I awaken the morning after a fatiguing exercise routine, I can *feel* achievement. Because the alternative is not appealing, I hope to continue this disciplined lifestyle.

If we are going to increase our spiritual strength we must expect opposition. The good news is, it's a fixed fight; the outcome has already been decided. Payment has been made in advance to ensure our victory. The bragging rival parading around the ring knows you are more than a conqueror.

Surviving Success

Basically satan is nothing more than a sparring partner who keeps us vigilant in the spirit. If we are not careful affluence will induce apathy. God refuses to let us become wealthy hobos—endowed with power but lacking spirit. We must walk circumspectly lest we become inebriated on prosperity.

The elderly warrior Caleb would not foster thoughts of a life of leisure in Canaan. Unfulfilled objectives had obsessed him for decades. His request was not to retire amid burgeoning meadows and nibble on luscious grapes. Instead he vigorously declared, "Give me this mountain" (see Josh. 14:12).

He knew exactly what was involved in such a decree: It meant war. Giants inhabited the mountain. The octogenarian could not retire knowing enemies populated part of his inheritance. With a youthful spirit, valiant faith, and an aged body, he achieved his goal.

Any measure of success can prove fatal if we desist short of absolute dominion. This is not about dividing real estate with adversaries so everyone can live in harmony. If you impart amnesty to an innocuous fiend, it will strengthen and emerge from dormancy with vicious retribution.

You can try to convince yourself that they are harmless denizens living in a remote region of your estate. They undoubtedly will be content to hibernate for a while. But when they awaken, they'll demand the entire parcel, not settle for a small portion. You can either deal with them now or dread them later.

A perfect example of this is when Saul was commanded to exterminate the Amalekites but instead spared their king, Agag (see 1 Sam. 15:9). Many years later a young Jewish maiden named Esther parried a conspiracy plotted by one of Agag's anti-Semitic descendants, Haman, to annihilate her people (see Esther 4–7).

Don't neglect those areas of your life that provide sanctuary for seditious attitudes. They'll scavenge off the algae of an impure heart and evolve into menacing imps. If you provide your enemy a foothold he'll turn it into a stronghold.

Neither give place to the devil (Ephesians 4:27).

The Winner's Epic

John Grisham is a talented man with a prolific mind. He has an extraordinary ability to hold his readers in absolute suspense. I might add that he is also quite powerful, to the point of life and death. Since he is the author, he gets to decide who will live and who will die. His scenarios are unpredictable but always end the way he intends them to.

While going through the trial of the millennium, Job said he wished his adversary had written a book (see Job 31:35). I think I understand Job's sentiment. Undoubtedly the devil would have written Job off a thousand times. But, you already know the rest of the story. As you read the first chapter of Job remember there's a 42nd chapter.

If the devil wants to keep footnotes on the events in my life, he can knock himself out. But he is not a novelist who gets to call the shots. He's whispered, "It's over" in my ear so many times that I refuse to acknowledge I've heard it. It's not up to him whether I live or die, or if I'm blessed or not. My Author is also my Finisher (see Heb. 12:2).

Perhaps you're in a free-fall nosedive toward certain doom. Satan has razed your world, causing irreparable damage. You inspect the vestiges of what was once your home; it has all been reduced to rubble.

You walk among the debris, confused and alone, petitioning God for a fragment of logic to this misfortune. Keep in mind, what you are experiencing is not the last chapter of your life. Keep reading! Before long you'll discover pages containing words such as health, laughter, and prosperity.

Satan has probably penned those two words of finality, *The End*, as he watches you sift through the cinders of what has been. He's making note of every expression and forming his own conclusions. Let him write what he may; it will be of no consequence to you.

God has already drafted the final pages of your life before you inhaled your first gulp of oxygen. He may have approved of a few hardships along the way, but not all mishaps are mistakes. Maybe we should regard them as uninvited agents sent to motivate us to greatness.

You and I don't expect to have our lives chronicled for the world to read. We certainly don't consider ourselves celebrities. But when God saved us, He inscribed our names in His catalogue of champions. Our responsibility is to *stay* in the book. We're the only ones capable of causing our names to be deleted.

One day the angel will place one foot on land and the other on the sea and declare that time shall be no more (see Rev. 10:5-6). As the 30 minutes of silence in Heaven expires, we'll probably stand there with mouths agape, ecstatic at what awaits (see Rev. 8:1). I expect to be approached by an elderly gentleman looking at me attentively and alleging, "I don't recall your name but I know I've seen your face before." Gladly I'll reply, "Yeah John, when you saw that crowd no man could count, I was in that number" (see Rev. 7:9).

In Deed—It's Yours

So, it's your first day in paradise and you're having a hard time growing accustomed to your new digs. You feel knee-high to a grasshopper and have no idea how you are going to conquest the country.

What is the first course of action to take upon meeting with opposition? I would suggest making a declaration. Find a piece of wood and sharpen one end. With the assistance of a heavy mallet, drive it into the ground. Square those shoulders, elevate that chin, and declare that you are here to stay. You elbowed your way through hell and high water, struggling to advance one inch at a time. You are not about to return to your scurrilous past.

You definitely are not going to formulate a compromise so you and your enemies can coexist. You are not a burglar heisting merchandise that belongs to someone else. You are reclaiming what was originally yours. Health and happiness were incorporated into the very foundation of your genesis.

This is not a temporary excursion from reality; this is now your homeland where you are going to reside permanently. You have to understand your rights! Satan will argue incessantly that you have no legal claim to stay. Just ignore him and commence setting up shop. He knows you're not an illegal alien. If you are born again the Bible is your proof of citizenship.

Going back is not an option. If you are contemplating doing so, you'll have to negotiate a method of forging those rushing currents. The God who divided the Jordan for your safe passage will not do so for your return. He is only involved in progression, not regression. I understand that you have interred some of your ancestry on the distant shore, but don't squander today by endeavoring to relive your past.

Satan is an intrusive archeologist who constantly attempts to exhume the relics of our former lives. We would do ourselves a great service by not revisiting these cemeteries that retain our decomposing corpses. There is a chance that we might divulge directions to satan when we tour around these old graveyards. Even God refuses to remember the route. There comes a time when you must give closure to yesterday and pursue tomorrow.

Brethren, I count not myself to have apprehended:
but this one thing I do, forgetting those things which

are behind, and reaching forth unto those things
which are before (Philippians 3:13).

You're not sure how li'l-ole-you is going to penetrate
these dense walls and subdue these giants. It's staggering to
realize all this has been deeded to you. You are not trespass-
ing; you are here claiming your inheritance.

You are the spiritual offspring of your father Abraham.
You haven't come to take sides; you have come to take over.
You're blessed going out, coming in, sitting down, standing
up, in the house, in the field, and in the city. You are from
above, not beneath; you are the head and not the tail, the
lender and not the borrower (see Gal. 3:7, Deut. 28:1-13).

Don't be intimidated by the lethal cache of weapons exhibited by your enemy. Regardless of their firepower, there is
not a single one that can prosper against you (see Is. 54:17).
Every round discharged from his muzzle will prove benign
and will not pose serious injury. You may obtain a few bruis-
es, but more obvious will be the one you embed on his head
from the sole of your foot.

Fear Factor

Don't cower in your Canaan, even though you feel like
you are aiming a pellet gun at a mighty military. Resist the
anxiety that is trying to immobilize you. This seemingly roar-
ing lion is actually a toothless feline. He may emit a blood-
curdling roar but there is not a solitary incisor in his mouth.

I am reminded of an attraction at Disney World that I
took my oldest daughter to see. Her sister didn't express any
interest in coming. On the other hand Datha was adamant in
experiencing the *Alien Encounter.*

As we waited in line for the doors to open, a voice came over the speakers saying something to the effect of: "If your body cannot handle electromagnetic energy, do not proceed." Of course this was a ploy to make the adventure a little more hair-raising. Datha could have left at that very moment feeling as though she had gotten her money's worth. But after she had dragged me across the entire Magic Kingdom, from Thunder Mountain Railroad to Toon Town, I wasn't about to leave without encountering this so-called alien.

We entered a theatre-like room and sat in seats that looked like they were engineered for the cockpit of an F16 fighter jet. The room became dark and someone began talking about capturing an alien creature. A spotlight revealed a glass cage close to the ceiling containing the most hideous beast you have ever seen.

This dude made the Loch Ness look like a gecko. It resembled something contrived in the mind of Stephen King. Roswell ain't never been visited by anything like this! Long bristly tentacles slithered along the interior of the enclosure. You know what Datha was thinking. "I hope that is double-plate glass!"

Lights went out, glass shattered, excitement could be heard in the announcer's voice, and Datha began inserting her fingernails into my forearm, pleading with me to get her out of there. That monster had broken loose and was somewhere close to where we were sitting, because I could feel its cold breath on the nape of my neck.

Before Datha became too frightened I took control of the situation by explaining that what she was witnessing was virtual reality. There was no extraterrestrial predator about to have us for supper. With the use of lenses, mirrors, and modern technology the projected image only appeared to be real.

We've never strolled down Main Street USA since, but should we return, I don't think we'll bother with another encounter with aliens. Was I terrified? Nope! I may have gotten a bit of a rush out of it. But I was aware it was an illusion. Had I believed it was real, I certainly wouldn't have taken my daughter where danger lurked.

God is apprised of what is real and what is bogus. He didn't drop us off on a distant planet with an unrestrained ferocious devil. I am not insinuating that satan is an imaginary sprite; I am just attempting to expose his true identity. He may behave like the bully on the block, but if you go toe-to-toe in the name of Jesus, he'll retreat in a hurry.

Submit yourselves therefore to God. Resist the devil,
and he will flee from you (James 4:7).

Stand firm on God's promises and look at the devil eyeball to eyeball. This fire-breathing dragon is a papier-mâché with a weak stomach at the sight of blood. Regardless of what some may think, satan is scared of blood. I guess you could say he's hemophobic. The Hollywood depictions of him associating with blood are false. When he commences his attack, revert to Calvary.

Clinging to the Cross

And the children of Israel encamped in Gilgal, and
kept the passover on the fourteenth day of the month

*at even in the plains of Jericho. And they did eat of
the old corn of the land on the morrow after the
passover, unleavened cakes, and parched corn in
the selfsame day* (Joshua 5:10-11).

Because the *passover* is symbolic of Christ's death, I am
suggesting that you celebrate the victory Christ accomplished
through His crucifixion, burial, and resurrection. We over-
come by the blood of the Lamb and the word of our testimony
(see Rev. 12:11).

If the enemy has raised his hideous head in some facet of
your life, causing discord, threatening to enslave your children, driving a wedge into your marriage, bringing financial
disaster, remind him of the blood.

Advise him that his final plummet will cause his descent
from Heaven to feel like an air pocket. When you are through
casting him out, pulling down strongholds, and releasing the
captives he has held hostage, it will require only one angel to
arrest him (see Rev. 20:1-3).

If you were impressed with the story of David and Goliath, get ready for some more amusing entertainment. The
devil is about to get his due. The sin and sickness he has dis-
persed upon humanity is coming home to haunt him.

I personally don't think it will require a Herculean angel
to slap the cuffs on satan and take him into custody. Neither
Michael nor Gabriel will be commissioned with the task. Perhaps there's an angel resembling Barney Fife, scrawny and
hyper, eager to experience action, but couldn't whip an egg,
whom God will deputize for the duty.

From Providence to Progress

And the manna ceased on the morrow after they had eaten of the old corn of the land; neither had the children of Israel manna any more; but they did eat of the fruit of the land of Canaan that year (Joshua 5:12).

The morning after the Passover the Israelites stepped out of their tents and never found as much as one white speck of manna again. When the manna stops descending that's when doubts start mounting.

Perhaps, figuratively speaking, this may be where you presently are in your spiritual expedition. This month the payment for the mortgage hasn't arrived. You invested your tithe and gave in the offering; now you say, "Show me the money." You purchased the property and paid for the plans and pledges have been promised, but now the bank is backing out.

Satan mocks you, suggesting you came all this way for nothing. You heard it was a land flowing with milk and honey, and now you look like a marooned moron. It's one thing to be in a foreign country and try to make sense of the menu, but now you're wondering, *Where is the menu?*

Pessimism takes advantage of the dire situation and lobs a salvo of skepticism on your beleaguered mind. Giants, impregnable entrenchment, and now this—no food. You are reluctant to think of what might confront you next. I understand God works on the cutting edge but this one is just a little too sharp.

Don't talk death. This is the land of your destiny, not your defeat. God didn't deliver you from iniquity just to have you die from malnutrition. Somewhere in the panorama there is sustenance just waiting to be consumed. You may not think it possible at this moment, but you are about to live better than you ever have.

It could be that God canceled the loan and is sending someone along to make a large deposit into your church treasury and not have you obligated to creditors. You don't have the imagination to propose a vision that God cannot afford to finance.

It is a most effective strategy of satan to have us standing at the doorway to world evangelism and waiting for someone to underwrite our expenses. We will not be exonerated in avowing insufficient funding impeded our doing the Master's bidding.

Read again Joshua 5:12 and find these words: "But they did eat." Open your mouth and proclaim: "I'm gonna eat! I will divide and conquer!" Heaven's holdings are not in receivership and thus God can no longer accommodate your needs. He has something far superior to manna in mind.

Memorializing the Miraculous

Throughout Israel's journeying through the wilderness, God kept admonishing them to remember it was He who liberated them from slavery. He also cautioned them not to forget Him when they entered the promised land.

We should make it our practice to memorialize those supernatural interventions that occur at the most desperate times of our lives. Not only will they serve as a testament to us but also to future generations (see Joshua 4:5-7).

It is crucial for us to visit the monuments of the miraculous that commemorate our pilgrimage from abject indigence to an abundant inheritance. That heap of stones didn't get there all by itself (see Josh. 4:6-7). The key to keeping a grip on God while handling blessings is to remember that He is the one responsible for everything we enjoy.

> *And it shall be, when the Lord thy God shall have brought thee into the land which He sware unto thy fathers, to Abraham, to Isaac, and to Jacob, to give thee great and goodly cities, which thou buildedst not, and houses full of all good things, which thou filledst not, and wells digged, which thou diggedst not, vineyards and olive trees, which thou plantedst not; when thou shalt have eaten and be full; then beware lest thou forget the Lord, which brought thee forth out of the land of Egypt, from the house of bondage* (Deuteronomy 6:10-12).

Understanding Adversity

I can sense that you're getting ahead of me and about to steal my thunder. I hope that faith is glancing off the recesses of your spirit like a golf ball bouncing on asphalt. You're beginning to see a reason for the irrational. Absurdity is making sense. The madness is losing its mystery.

So that's why God permitted the adversary to live in your promised land. Remember those cold nights when you lay shivering under a tent while your enemy was sleeping in a house constructed with stone. For 40 years you wore the same clothes. Instead of God breathing life into the material, why didn't He provide a change of wardrobe? Manna nearly drove you bananas!

When it appeared that the enemy was living the good life, he was actually building your life. That's not his house, or his garden, or his vineyard, or his well. God saw you coming and allowed an enemy to make preparations for your arrival.

How is your year going thus far? Have you been involved in an unusual amount of wrestling? Are areas of your life giving you difficulty that never posed the slightest problem in the past? Is your ministry under a barrage of aggression from internal and external forces? Has your business suddenly contracted a deadly virus and there is no prognosis for survival? Has your home changed from being the little house on the prairie to the flustered home of the dreary?

Go ahead and tell the devil, "Build my house, plant my garden, dress my vineyard, and dig my well." You're in pursuit of claiming your stuff! You may be meek but one should not mistake your humility for timidity. You've come a long way and it's either blessings or bust. An understanding of adversity has quickened your spirit and you are not about to abandon your promise.

Appreciating Adversity

You not only lived your life with him; you lived your life for him. You earned meager wages working in unpleasant surroundings, enabling him to attend university and further his education. Along with his masters he acquired a mistress.

Irreconcilable differences beached your luxury liner laden with marital bliss on the jagged shores of divorce. The handsome beau who stole your heart handed it back to you in pieces. The fairy tale wedding became another sad statistic.

Eight years earlier you were a valedictorian with scholarships to Ivy League institutions. Instead of pursuing your own goals you forfeited your future so he could prepare for his. Unfortunately you have been abruptly eliminated from the one you fantasized of sharing with him. Reality has made a disheartening intrusion. You had no idea emotional pain could be so severe.

The misery has faded into a memory and life isn't so bad. God heard you on your knees and sent a gentleman who swept you off your feet. Your mind has received contentment, your heart has discovered true love, and your soul has experienced absolute fulfillment.

You have a new spouse who is faithful and a new faith that is dependable in a God who is infallible. You are a recipient of spiritual renewal. When your world disintegrated you reverted to the God of your childhood and were enveloped in His unchanging compassion. The reality of His presence in your life has inspired a devotion you never possessed.

You find yourself daily lingering at His feet and ingesting His Word into your spirit. Prayer is no longer the equivalent of a root canal now that you have developed a personal relationship with Christ. Your Bible has become your source of encouragement and church has become a way of life.

I understand that the hypothesis I am proposing is stretching the delicate fabric of rationality, but perhaps in some diminutive way we are indebted to the devil. Don't get upset; ponder it for a moment. You may be thinking, *If you only knew the half of the anguish I have had to endure.* Forgive me if I seem insensitive, but you made it! Now here's my question: Would you be where you presently are and know God in such intimacy if the circumstances were different?

I am not implying that the previously stated events are unavoidable. Marriages don't have to bust up to have God break in. I am simply illustrating how when one is shoved into the doleful closet of depression God's glory can illuminate the most deplorable circumstances. The end result can produce a relationship with God that never before existed. One doesn't have to become ill to know that God is a healer. But when the Great Physician restores health to your languishing body, it engenders a faith you never knew.

The Miracle Is in Your Mouth

Prayer and fasting won't produce manna when God says, "No more." Arguing that you have done it a certain way all your life will not generate a solitary grain of the heavenly bread either. Don't waste your time trying to recreate an era that God has abandoned.

This is a new day with a new way. Things are different on this side of the river. The monotonous routine of yesterday has ceased. You will not have to gather your provisions at daybreak before pests invade them. Fruitful acres of agriculture are available at any time.

> God is waiting on you to announce it; then He will accomplish it. You can have it, if you really want it, but you have to demand it.

Your first crop has already been planted and if you will sow a small percentage of your harvest you will never suffer want. Preserve a modest portion to be used for seed and not for feed.

This is an opportunity to invest in your future with absolutely no risk and yet have lucrative returns. Tithing is the financial formula that God has instituted for your sustained success.

God sometimes alters the way He blesses so we can experience a new level of authority. The purpose for the drastic change was for your promotion. The creative power of the Word now lives inside you. God is waiting on you to announce it; then He will accomplish it. You can have it, if you really want it, but you have to demand it.

> But what saith it? The word is nigh thee, even in thy mouth, and in thy heart: that is, the word of faith, which we preach (Romans 10:8).

You're not going to get to eat by picking up, but by speaking up. Stop waiting for a spiritual superhero to come along and vanquish the enemies who inhabit your promises. There are some things that God has intended for us to accomplish on our own.

You ought to exhale Holy Spirit authority like the exhaust from a 747 at full throttle. Tell your adversary his lease on the land has lapsed and to relinquish everything that God intended for you to possess.

It's time to make your move. You don't have to bring a thing; all has been provided by a most unexpected benefactor. Satan is not exactly what you would consider a patron saint, but he served your purpose well. He is a slow learner with a terrible memory. He can never seem to remember that calamity becomes a gateway to destiny.

> That the trial of your faith, being much more precious than of gold that perisheth, though it be

*tried with fire, might be found unto praise and ho-
nour and glory at the appearing of Jesus Christ*
(1 Peter 1:7).

Chapter Six

LOSING YOUR EDGE

And the sons of the prophets said unto Elisha, Behold now, the place where we dwell with thee is too strait for us. Let us go, we pray thee, unto Jordan, and take thence every man a beam, and let us make us a place there, where we may dwell. And he answered, Go ye. And one said, Be content, I pray thee, and go with thy servants. And he answered, I will go. So he went with them. And when they came to Jordan, they cut down wood. But as one was felling a beam, the axe head fell into the water: and he cried, and said, Alas, master! for it was borrowed. And the man of God said, Where fell it? And he showed him the place. And he cut down a stick, and cast it in thither; and the iron did swim. Therefore said he, Take it up to thee. And he put out his hand, and took it (2 Kings 6:1-7).

We have arrived at the concluding chapter in our literary journey and together we have traipsed through throes and prose and relived some dramatic events. In some instances I granted myself liberty in conveying austere analysis, while in others less caustic subjects were articulated. I trust the satirical and solemn achieve symmetry.

This has been an exhausting marathon but we are finally sprinting down the last mile. I pray that you have been inspired and that your earnest desire to know God more intimately has been elevated to a higher dimension.

I am very much aware that this book will be but a mouthful of nourishment to your hungry heart. As I have wrenched and squeezed my spirit to extract every drop of inspiration, you have been devouring every edible morsel you could forage to edify your soul.

Although we've never been formally introduced, it is apparent you and I share a common interest. We possess an inexorable determination to converge upon Christ and acquire His inestimable attributes. Tasting and seeing that the Lord is good engenders a holy addiction. We find ourselves codependent on His presence.

Once again, writing has elicited varied emotions, the majority of which are associated with anxiety. Finding the right words doesn't come easily to me; I compare it to bobbing for apples in Lake Superior. It is essential that I be constantly armed with a pen to seize that one thought that makes an abbreviated appearance from some secluded niche of my heart.

Each book creates a void and this emptiness always produces empathy for authors: the imaginative people who stretch their minds and deplete their resources to inscribe their very souls on paper.

I have crunched on the keyboard of my laptop in airport terminals, at least a dozen hotel rooms, two summer cottages, and now I have retreated to the back of my house, where my office is located. The atmosphere is quiet but my mind is restless and I wonder if my best is good enough.

I actually borrowed my wife's favorite seat in the house and moved it in here; it's much more comfortable than the one behind my desk. It took me three trips to carry the floral print armchair, cushions, and ottoman. I have to meet tomorrow's deadline and overnight the manuscript to the real professionals who will clean it up and make me look smart.

Next week I am going to shut down the computer and pull the golf clubs out from mothballs. It's a small stimulus I have promised myself after not having any recreation for the last several months. In case you're wondering, my golfing is worse than my writing. "Fore" is a word I frequently shout on the course.

I want to express my gratitude for the honor you have bestowed on me in selecting this book. You have afforded me something that is priceless—your time—which places me in your debt. Thank you for allowing me to make a modest contribution in your spiritual expedition. I hope I have been an enlightening companion.

Forgive me if I am imposing, but I have a request to ask of you: Please ensure this book, with emphasis on this chapter, lands in the hands of someone to whom the subject matter is relevant—a minister fallen from grace, or perhaps reeling from exhaustion; the young rookie beginning his ministry, but tormented with feelings of failure; a new Christian struggling with carnality, convinced he will never get back on his feet; a teenager sidetracked by sin, needing a way back home; an unappreciated housewife daily investing long hours of labor in her home. Being a stay-at-home mom is an unpopular occupation in today's politically correct society; she may be contemplating the merits of her role.

Probably by now a name has come to mind: someone in your own family, or circle of friends, who is feeling forlorn. I pray as I relay the story of a young ministerial acquaintance, as well as the distressed son of a prophet, faith will arise from a discouraged heart. The compassionate heart of our heavenly Father anxiously waits to restore what sin or perhaps frustration has stolen.

I would like for you and me to make a pact to rescue our perishing comrades who have been wounded in combat. Let's become intercessors who straddle two opposing stratums and resist demonic warmongers, who seek to capture the blood-stained bodies of our fellow soldiers, drag them to their dingy lairs, and complete their wicked intentions.

Whenever I minister, I always end the sermon by offering atonement. If this was not the case, I believe I would commit an inexcusable atrocity. And thus is my strategy in *Magnificent Meekness*. My compensation for months of laborious writing will be to have you submit a testimony of redemption to my wonderful publisher, Destiny Image, or to me. I will be elated beyond definition to learn of a wounded comrade who has undergone total recovery. So, with this in mind, let's begin our final moments together.

Debilitating Disparity

I listened intently, my heart immersed with emotion, as the young pastor described in painstaking detail the spiritual drought he had experienced. He related how he felt the anointing had been permanently removed from him. He endured several months of services by simply going through the mechanics.

It didn't require being in his presence very long to realize he was a born leader. He embodied limitless potential and, considering he had only been in the ministry a few years, had experienced a considerable measure of success.

He had a unique way of articulating his thoughts and always maintained the attention of his audience. After being full-time for only a matter of months, his reputation spread quickly throughout his denomination, which produced numerous invitations for speaking engagements. Everywhere he ministered, people spoke highly of him and recommended him to their friends.

He never met a stranger and seemed to win over everyone he met. He had developed a strong rapport with the clergy in his town and officiated at various municipal functions. Basically, he was a people-magnet thanks to an irresistible personality.

His star was rising rapidly with no indication of slowing down. He wasn't reluctant to accept a challenge and always aimed for the sky. He was a depository for information, constantly ingesting information and improving his skills.

By all accounts he was a success. His wife was enjoying the perks and privileges connected to a successful up-and-coming pastor. His church had tripled in membership, and plans were being made to relocate to a larger facility.

When he had originally assumed the pastorate the congregation consisted of only a few, mostly disgruntled, members. The financial status was pitiful. It seemed as if every business in the small town was sending monthly statements, requesting payment be made in full. This can cause irreparable damage, as well as incite unwanted publicity, which had been the case here.

The church facility had been dilapidated; several thousand dollars were needed just to bring the sanctuary to any kind of acceptable level. The former pastor had not been a visionary, and had not established plans for growth. So, they were assembling in a run-down, humid, overcrowded auditorium.

Fortunately, this young fireball was a breath of fresh air to a congregation who felt their best days were at their back. He was innovative, personable, and his family reflected his attributes. He was a godsend. From his first sermon as new pastor to present, he never slackened. Counseling, praying, planning, fund-raising, and personal evangelism: He did them all sacrificing precious family time, and pouring himself into the work of God.

On Fire But Burning Out

Unfortunately, he failed to pay attention to the continual drain on his resources. In reality, he was his own worst enemy. He felt guilty whenever he and his family slipped out of town for a few days for a little reprieve from the daily grind. He was confronted with problems and opposition, especially from those of the old-school mentality, who opposed his methods. But he kept it inside, not wanting to be perceived as weak, which is the case with a lot of us in leadership.

A vacuum was slowly developing internally. His attitude was not longsuffering, at home or at church. His negligence toward his wife and children was putting distance between them. As he worked diligently to influence a community and increase a church, the chasm between him and his family kept widening. His wife was beginning to resent his absence. When he was home, his attention was divided, and his family was always at the short end of the stick. Telephone calls interrupted every single meal.

As all of this drama played out, satan was subtly laying a trap. It almost worked. The young pastor allowed himself to get into a compromising situation that would have produced a disastrous aftermath. However, someone must have interceded in prayer. An act of sin did not occur. He salvaged his family, ministry, and church. Today he continues to be a successful leader of a vibrant, ever-increasing congregation.

Sooner or later we will all encounter the inevitable. We will rub shoulders with exhaustion and be solicited by temptation. Satan will levy accusations and attempt to smear our credibility. Lurking in the shadows of every man and woman of God is a demon devising a pitfall to destroy their credibility.

It was painful, as well as extremely humiliating for him to relive this closed chapter in his life. As he spoke I could detect apprehension in his voice. Perhaps he was wondering if his disclosure had jeopardized our relationship. Perceiving this to be the case, I took the initiative and reaffirmed my covenant with him.

A friend is someone to whom you can spill your guts and he won't spill the beans. He'll never turn your confession into a machete and butcher you with your own words. When your detractors are spreading rumors you can be certain he's stamping them out.

Whenever I meet up with this young pastor, he locks me in a warm embrace and thanks me for my friendship. I don't feel superior or more spiritual than him, but instead I understand I will obligate his friendship somewhere along the way.

Illustrated Hopelessness

I'm not sure that there is another passage in the Bible that depicts utter hopelessness more graphically than the story in Second Kings. I have pored over these Scriptures several times but have seldom preached from them until one day it became much more than ink on India paper. I was able to perceive a desperate young man who had lost his edge.

I don't expect the entire readership community to be awestruck as if some abysmal revelatory knowledge has just been imparted to them. However, I do feel a mandate of the Holy Spirit to include a message of hope in this offering.

It is my feeling that within the Body of Christ there is an enormous amount of hurting that slips by somewhat unnoticed. I am well aware that as I write this chapter there are numerous ministers and laity who are standing on the precipice of disaster and about to become another statistic.

I personally believe that spiritual warfare is a vital element in our quest to reach a world full of lost humanity. We are engaged in a ferocious battle with the forces of darkness, and satan is not relenting. I also feel, as we continue to harvest fresh fields, that it is time to become introspective and minister to those among us who are a breath away from spiritual extinction. There are maimed ministers occupying pulpits and suffering saints sitting in pews who are becoming increasingly ill. The prophet Jeremiah was right on the money when he wrote:

> *Is there no balm in Gilead; is there no physician there? why then is not the health of the daughter of my people recovered?* (Jeremiah 8:22)

It has been said that as Napoleon was endeavoring to gain world dominance, he held a world globe in his hands and ran his fingertips over the rough terrain of China, uttering these famous words: "China is a sleeping giant, woe unto the world when she awakes." I would like to paraphrase the deceased tyrant: "The Church is a sleeping giant, woe unto the kingdom of darkness when she awakes."

If the Church would stir from her slumber and become reconnected to the needs of

Weak areas of our lives don't have to evolve into malignancies that are like deadly assassins taking aim on their next victim.

those within her own walls, hell would encounter its worst nightmare. We all need to attain a level of honesty that would allow us to disclose to a covenant partner when we are hurting or feel totally washed up. Weak areas of our lives don't have to evolve into malignancies that are like deadly assassins taking aim on their next victim.

Why, when we feel ineffective, do we always respond with the same old rhetoric, "Everything's just great"—when inside frigid wisps of air circulate through the alcoves of our spirit, where once an ardent flame ignited our soul? Maybe it is because we rub shoulders with spiritual titans and we cannot afford to appear weak or unsuccessful.

Satan is a devil of a devil. He's the best at being bad. He stalks us from our first postnatal moment and all through life to seduce us into one of his sinister schemes. Then, when we fail, he pounces mercilessly on us, constantly reminding us of this failure.

Then of course satan tabulates higher points when we who belong to the same platoon *talk about* instead of *travail for* our wounded comrade. Could it be that at times we are more interested in the circumstances than the consequences? Negative news of fallen associates moves rapidly through the chatter conduit, carrying with it the sordid details.

Will Someone Call a Doctor?

What if the Church was a little less pontificating, pompous, and judgmental, and every member became a courier for clemency? When news of someone in peril reaches our ears we should spontaneously fall to our knees and plead for his or her redemption. If we can't even appreciate each other, how can we ever rescue each other?

May we never be indicted for negligence by overlooking casualties molested by this world, but instead become impassioned with the charitable spirit of the Good Samaritan. Our places of worship must be "cities of refuge," not judicial forums for zealous prosecutors to hold tribunals.

Our criminal justice system has implemented a "three strikes" program before the felon is incarcerated indefinitely. Surely we as Christians can, at the very least, offer an open heart instead of recommending swift punishment before a hearing commences.

Dismantling the church government that God has instituted would not be prudent. We need accountability and spiritual elders to discipline and direct us. Reproof and rebuke are essential elements of restoration. What I am suggesting is seeking out those who are wounded or feel burned out and rendering proper aid until recovery is complete.

The revelatory gifts of the Spirit are not weapons to inflict injury, but rather implements to administer healing and restoration. Our objective must always be to edify and never to embarrass. It is imperative that we extend an open hand and not a clenched fist: "Blessed are the merciful: for they shall obtain mercy" (Mt. 5:7).

The church is not a dim-lit interrogation room where one is finally broken down through intimidation and threats, and eventually confesses to a transgression. If only the flawless were granted membership, who would attend?

If Thou, Lord, shouldest mark iniquities, O Lord, who shall stand? (Psalm 130:3)

Absent But Not Extinct

In the Scriptures that preface our chapter, we find a group of young men zealous in the Lord's work. Their Bible-school dormitory is too small. The quarters are cramped and it is time to expand. If you're going to have a problem, this is a good one to have. The Kingdom of God should be continuously progressing and not regressing. Also, I think everyone who has attended a Bible college or seminary shares the sentiments of these young men who approached Elisha. We've all thought, at one time or another, of our roommates as space invaders.

In a united effort they all go down to the Jordan River and begin hewing down trees. So much for, "I was called to preach and prophecy, not to be a lumberjack!" Calluses will not impede the laying on of hands! A little manual labor won't impair your heavenly calling!

As the process of cutting down the timber was underway, one of the young men lost his axe head. Physics is not my forte, but I do understand a couple laws that come into play in this event. It's a lost cause! The axe head is history! With the weight of iron verses the weight of water, it's over!

Another point worthy of noting is that the Jordan was a muddy, murky river. Unlike the rivers of Eastern Canada, where I fished as a boy, the Jordan didn't flow with water clear enough to see the bottom. You can't find what can't be seen.

The axe head was lost but not gone! It had disappeared from sight but not from existence! I want to emphasize this fact until it penetrates your cranium and continues into your spirit. The enemy of your soul relentlessly reminds you that you have lost your effectiveness for good. The logistics and dynamics surrounding your situation are self-explanatory. It is as clear as the axe handle you are holding. The muddy waters of despair have enclosed around the anointing you once had. You no longer are participating with your peers in the work of the Lord.

The Work of God Versus the Will of God

The young man in this passage did not lose his edge over idleness. He was not a slothful servant. He flexed his muscles, gripped the axe, and wielded the keen edge into the bark of the tree. He lost it while doing what he was supposed to be doing. If he lacked anything, perhaps it was vigilance. As beads of perspiration accumulated on his brow, the axe head began to vibrate on the handle. It slowly made its way over the top before the lad became aware there was a problem.

I have been guilty of doing the work of God more than the will of God. Cramming extra meetings into an already crowded itinerary! Agreeing to minister at several conferences on top of weekly crusades. My luggage is never completely unpacked before it is tagged for another flight.

As a result of this there have been times I felt my effectiveness begin to wane. My preaching schedule was full but my prayer life was deteriorating. There is something of much greater importance than being in demand as a conference speaker. As someone once admonished me, "When you're riding the crest, keep your eyes focused in all directions." Things that seem trivial can be lethal.

Walking the straight and narrow does not suggest a tightrope. If you feel you are performing a perilous balancing act, it is time to descend the ladder. Cheering crowds are not worth losing your life. The higher you ascend the more conscientious you must become. Altitudes can play havoc on one's depth perception.

Jesus' ministry spanned three-and-a-half years, and yet He took time to withdraw from the masses to pray and rest.

Perhaps, figuratively speaking, we cannot come to the garden while the dew is still on the roses because we live in a concrete jungle. We have no time to smell the flowers because we must tend crops. Responsibilities demand we take care of our fields, but if we don't stroll through a garden once in a while, we may not survive to harvest the crop!

Is there a lesson here? Absolutely! If we overwork our fields and ourselves, we will empty both of the vital nutrients essential for production.

That is precisely why the Lord instructed the children of Israel in agriculture. They were to sow and reap for six years but refrain on the seventh. The field needed a rest to be refreshed. Humanity was created from the dust of the earth. We were commanded to rest every seventh day (see Ex. 23:10-12)! Is there a lesson here? Absolutely! If we overwork our fields and ourselves, we will empty both of the vital nutrients essential for production.

It Never Hurts to Ask

Your successful days are not all at your back, regardless if you are a young minister feeling burnout or a seasoned saint feeling worn out. A few years ago my wife and I, along with some friends, were visiting Korea. We decided to do a little shopping in Etawon.

As we made our way through the crowded streets, nodding to vendors soliciting tourists to purchase their wares, I realized that my camera was no longer with me. It was a simple

Canon Rebel 35mm, not something that would require a computer science degree from MIT to operate. Although it cost less than $300, its sentimental value was much greater because it had accompanied me around the world.

Retracing my steps, I inquired about the camera in all the shops we had entered, but to no avail. The gentleman traveling with me advised me to write it off. In a city of over eight million people, the chances of recovering it were slim to none.

When we arrived back at the hotel around 4:00 p.m., I mentioned my loss to the concierge. In less than an hour I received a call inviting me to pick up my camera in the atrium of the hotel. The concierge had checked with all the cabdrivers servicing hotel patrons until he located the one we had used. The driver had placed my camera in the trunk of his cab.

I know it seems irretrievable but your buried talent is worth inquiring about. If you will never be in possession of it again, pray tell, why is satan so adamant in reminding you it is gone for good? Here is a five-step program to recovery:

1

Don't go home without it!

Regardless of how impossible your circumstances are, don't go home empty-handed. When everything around is declaring defeat, hang around. Although you may not be assisting your associates, you are much better off in their company than with a group of unbelievers. Your environment will have a profound effect on you, so be sure to maintain one that is healthy. Don't consort with someone who suffered a loss and surrendered to despair. Their pessimism will smother any optimism of restoration.

Their venomous words will embitter your mind and before long you will acquire the martyr's spirit: thinking everyone is out to get you. Your thinking will become distorted and make you believe your colleagues are a lynch mob carrying a noose, when in reality they are rescuers throwing you a lifeline. You may have lost confidence in yourself, but try and maintain a little faith in others.

Don't become a recluse and refuse to be around those who want to restore you. You may have let them down, but please let them in. Don't allow shame to force you into seclusion. You may feel completely useless and ineffective and more of a liability than anything. But they don't mind picking up the slack and pinch-hitting.

The reason they are so persistent in making contact with you is because they cannot allow you to be discarded on the scrap heap. You are a member of the Body of Christ in need of encouragement. Don't make an automatic deduction that when your name comes up in conversation, it is in a negative context. They are trying to salvage you so you are not excised from the Body.

It's true; the Church does have more than its quota of talebearers. However, there are still those who would step into the fiery flames of hell with a squirt gun and demand your immediate release. Should enemy ammo knock you off your feet, they'll jeopardize their lives to carry your blood-soaked body to safety.

A friend loveth at all times, and a brother is born for adversity (Proverbs 17:17).

2
Confess that you lost it!

Denial only works so long. Going through the mechanics will not produce positive results. Without the axe head you are simply striking wood against wood as one beating the air. If you felt tired before, you are about to experience exhaustion. You may be swinging, but the tree is still standing, and nothing is being accomplished. If you keep operating with a headless axe you will undoubtedly encounter burnout. And this presents another set of problems.

You draft inspiring sermons and expound eloquently, but the captivating efficacy of the Holy Spirit is not present. You extend your arms to Heaven, shouting hallelujahs and speaking in languages of men and of angels, but all is sounding brass and tinkling cymbals. Your singing is professional but not persuasive. His awesome glory no longer comforts the hearts of the congregation as you exalt Him through your talent.

> If you keep operating with a headless axe you will undoubtedly encounter burnout. And this presents another set of problems.

You remember the day when the anointing of the Holy Spirit elevated you into a higher dimension and everyone in attendance was aware that another world had descended. Accompanying the Glory were the cherubim, and it seemed as though one could sense the brush of angels' wings. You recall the day when you were sharp in the Spirit and could sever enemy shackles. A mere whisper of His incomparable Name caused rebel forces to recoil in terror.

Don't make a rash decision and throw in the towel because you no longer can be a benefit to the cause. It makes no difference whether you are a new convert who has stumbled or a medal-bearing veteran feeling tired and out of touch. Swallow your pride and admit there is something missing from your life.

Acknowledge immediately what will become apparent to everyone: Something essential is absent.

3
Confide in someone spiritual!

Brethren, if a man be overtaken in a fault, ye which are spiritual, restore such an one in the spirit of meekness; considering thyself, lest thou also be tempted (Galatians 6:1).

Confiding in the wrong source may annul any hope of ever seeing the axe head again. Be sure your counselor is an advocate, not an accuser. You need one to speak *for* you, not *against* you. Don't be presumptuous in thinking no one has ulterior motives. Go to someone known for spending time on their knees and not on the phone. If any of your acquaintances have a history of being a human telegraph, remember, just because they slap you on the back doesn't mean they won't stab you in the back.

Confidence in an unfaithful man in time of trouble is like a broken tooth, and a foot out of joint (Proverbs 25:19).

Be certain he or she is a person of faith and believes in restoration. There are naysayers who do not believe in the supernatural power of the Spirit and thus will try and dissuade you. Go to someone who has radical faith and believes with God anything is possible.

I am not amazed that Elisha would ask the young man, "Where fell it?" After all he is the prophet endowed with the double portion. He has extreme faith! That is why he rebuked Joash for only smiting the arrows on the ground three times when he should have done it six times; Joash cut his miracle in half (see 2 Kings 13:15-19). Elisha's mindset was not to get along but to get everything.

Don't heed the advice of someone who, when hearing of the missing blade, will chuckle, pat you on the shoulder, and suggest you call it a day and go on home and apply for another job. That is why this young generation of believers must have access to elders who still believe in the miraculous! The voice of wisdom, conditioned through time, encourages us to hope when everything appears hopeless.

Solicit the guidance of an intercessor, someone who will enter into agreement and stay with you until complete recovery is gained. We desperately need a resurgence of the prophetic in our midst; a seer who can point us in the right direction whether we lost our father's goats like Saul, or an axe head like this lad.

4

Return to where you lost it!

When was the last time you felt the anointing? When was the first time you noticed a void in your life? You cannot proceed onward until you go backward. The memories may be painful, but blocking it out of your mind will only decrease your chances of coming into contact with the missing object.

Don't settle for a counterfeit! You know the real thing when you see it! Hold out for the genuine that has yoke-destroying power. Don't buy the enemy's lie that you can never be used of the Lord again. The fact that you failed doesn't make you a failure. So, you took a few swings and nothing happened. Losing your edge doesn't make you a loser! You have been reminded once again that your broad shoulders and muscular forearms cannot fell the tree without the acute anointing of the Holy Spirit.

Remember those early days of dedication? The days you fasted and prayed! You lay before the Lord and requested that He search every chamber of your heart! Return to the consecration of your youth.

You will not find it at conferences and camp meetings, but rather in your closet. You may rationalize that a geographic change will rekindle your spirit. The missing edge is not across the seven seas, it's somewhere on the bottom of the muddy river at your feet!

5

Pick it up!

Phenomenal events often occurred at the Jordan. A great deal of history aligns the banks of this 200-mile river. Initiate a little Q & A with Joshua, Elisha, and Naaman; they'll share their exceptional testimonies of God's blessings.

Jordan simply means "descending"! It is synonymous with spiritual enterprise. Wait on its bank, something miraculous is about to happen! I understand that you cannot see the axe head, let alone touch it. It is somewhere on the floor of the ocean of despair, covered in mire.

The bugle may be playing taps, and friends may have already composed an appropriate eulogy. However, no wreaths will be laid at your burial plot today. It is my opinion that God included this story in His Bible to inform you it's not over until it's over. Elisha threw a branch into the water and the axe head swam. Physicists declare it impossible! Gravity and Mother Nature are working against you! Your adversary is ruthless in his barrage of missiles aimed at your mind!

What you can't see or touch is coming to you! God will breathe life into the defunct ministry, demand it to surface from the murky depths and swim back into your hands. You need not so much as roll up the bottoms of your britches and get your toes wet. Your part is easy—reach out and take it! Reach out with an arm of faith and take hold of that which was lost. Seize it tightly, and don't ever lose sight of it again.

This has been an educational experience you will never forget. Each time you brandish the blade, you will be watchful and make sure it is fastened securely. The episode has reminded you that you are effective only if you are anointed!

You have not experienced your last anointing! The waters of despair cannot retain that which God has ordained for you to have. The enemy can't keep what only God can give. The frozen atmosphere enveloping you is thawing out. Once again you will be a minister who is a flaming fire.

Once again you will sing with anointing, and as the audience worships, Heaven will applaud. The Shekinah will fill the sanctuary, inhibiting protocol from being a priority. Fresh fervor will engulf your spirit as hallelujahs ascend from your heart.

Alas, Master! For It Was Borrowed

Is all this too far out for you? Sound too sensational? Just answer this question: Whose anointing was it to begin with? That which you lost was not yours in the first place! We may say, "*my* gift, *my* anointing, *my* ministry"; but it all belongs to Him. They are tools that help us accomplish the will of God more efficiently.

> *Every good gift and every perfect gift is from above,*
> *and cometh down from the Father of lights, with*
> *whom is no variableness, neither shadow of turning*
> (James 1:17).

Take a stroll down memory lane to where God first called you. You considered yourself the least of the least. When the Holy Spirit nominated you for service in the Kingdom, you replied that you were inadequate. Surely there was a misprint and your name was placed in the wrong category. You were supposed to be on the list of those most likely to be a nobody. There was no clerical error; God branded you for service. From that moment you became a marked man.

The Eternal God of glory who spoke worlds into existence never uttered the phrase *uh-oh*! Never has the Lord said *oops*! His Word is His expression, and just like Him it is infallible. You're not a mistake; you're a miracle.

I have a question: Is it harder for God to restore your anointing than it was to give it in the first place? Take a moment and think. Uh-huh, my thoughts exactly! So why stand there empty-handed?

All around you there are numerous illustrations of the miraculous. It's not Mother Nature but rather Father God who sustains life and keeps all of creation in harmony. They are not the coincidental results of evolving life forms. They are the handiwork of an infinite God.

- An eagle builds a nest a certain size to accommodate its mate and eaglets. The sparrow accumulates twigs and straw and weaves its nest. They never get confused and build one suited for another species.

- A salmon swims through estuaries and tributaries, arriving in the vast ocean. After traveling thousands of miles in its lifetime, the fish instinctively navigates its way back to the exact spot where it was hatched and there it dies.

- A fuzzy, repulsive caterpillar spins a cocoon, enters, and awaits change. The metamorphosis takes place and out flies a graceful Monarch Butterfly on delicate, velvety wings.

- The soil parts and a stem emerges. The bud blooms and another delightful creation appears. Untouched by human hands, the pedals unfold to liberate the brilliance and fragrance of the rose.

- An unremitting prevaricator became a Holy Ghost preacher and witnessed an unprecedented revival. The mouth that once denied Christ preached at Pentecost and thousands were saved.

- A boy just so happened to be born the nineteenth child, which today is not considered rational. As a lad he was scrawny and homely; as a teen he was the biggest nerd in town, introverted, and limited in opportunity. And you are reading his book!

Now, what was it you were considering impossible? He found you in the dark alley of a street called *nowhere*, wasted on sin and discouraged with life. You were the poster-boy for the Institution of the Morally Bankrupt and given a lifetime membership.

There were no exit signs providing escape from the contaminated atmosphere of your licentious lifestyle. Like an abscessed stomach on a starvation diet, your emaciated soul ached for relief. What was it you were shackled by? How eerie were those sleepless nights?

Someone delivered news that just had to be too good to be true. Why would an innocent Man give his life for a loser like you? Since your life was colliding into a dead end and you had no better place to go, you went. At the foot of the cross you knelt and unloaded a lifetime of pain.

You weren't eligible to inhabit a dumpster, but suddenly admission was granted for you to stroll into the luxurious atrium of the royal residence. You not only were furnished with private quarters, you were given the keys to the entire Kingdom. The day before, you were busted, disgusted, and couldn't be trusted and then, overnight, unlimited affluence was at your disposal.

This stroll through the dim-lit corridors of retrospection is serving a purpose. You smile and weep as you reminisce of a despairing past. Before and after images appear in your mind and the transformation is staggering. So, it was miraculous after all when God anointed you! Jump to your feet! Hurry on down to the muddy river's bank. Supernatural power is resurrecting your gift.

You don't have to wade into the clouded waters of despair. The Jordan River is accustomed to authority, regardless if the command is to open up or give it up. It rolled back for the feet of priests and the mantle of a prophet. I know you're feeling dry and disconnected, but just toss that dead branch in and watch something living come out. Come back and join us as we strive to expand God's Kingdom.

Should God grant me another opportunity to spend time with you, I'll accept the invitation; you're great company. As you lay down the book, I'll put back the chair. Before I select save on my menu, I'll leave you with a word from the wise, the apostle Paul. He was quite a piece of work when you think of it!

For the gifts and calling of God are without repentance (Romans 11:29).

ENDNOTES

1. Bennett, William J., *The Broken Hearth* (New York, NY: Doubleday and WaterBrook Press, divisions of Random House, Inc., 2001) p. 69.

2. Ibid, p. 70.

3. Meier, Paul D.; Wichem, Frank; Minirth, Frank; Ratcliff, Donald; *Introduction to Psychology and Counseling*, 2nd ed. (Grand Rapids, MI: Baker Book House, 1991) pp. 249, 251.

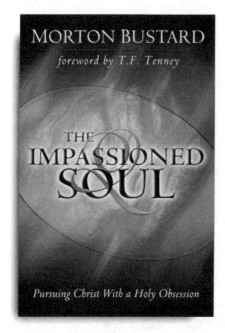

THE IMPASSIONED SOUL
By Morton Bustard

What mysterious force lifts a person out of the mainstream of mediocrity into the lonely pursuit of the heavenly vision? It is *passion*. Passion is the energy of the soul and the fire of life. Passion leads you to a life that will end the drought in your inner being. *The Impassioned Soul* comes to you as a cup of cool water for the thirsty pursuer. As its refreshing words touch your scorched soul, you will feel the energy of its life revitalizing all the parched places.

ISBN: 0-7684-2113-6

For more information regarding Morton Bustard's ministry, visit his website at **www.mortonbustard.com**